Nothing's Impossible

Lorraine Monroe

NOTHING'S IMPOSSIBLE

LEADERSHIP LESSONS FROM
INSIDE AND OUTSIDE THE CLASSROOM

PublicAffairs
NEW YORK

Published by PublicAffairs™, a member of the Perseus Books Group.

Book design by Jenny Dossin.

Reprinted by arrangement with Times Books, a division of Random House, Inc.

Library of Congress Cataloging-in-Publication Data

Monroe, Lorraine.
    Nothing's impossible : leadership lessons from inside and outside
the classroom / Lorraine Monroe. —
1st PublicAffairs ed.
        p.   cm.
    Originally published: New York : Times Books, c1997.
    Includes index.
    ISBN-13 978-1-891620-20-1 (pbk.) ISBN-10 1-891620-20-7 (pbk.)
    1. Monroe, Lorraine.   2. Frederick Douglass Academy (Harlem, New York,
N.Y.)   3. Educational leadership—New York (State)—New York. 4. School
improvement programs—New York (State)—New York.   5. Afro-American
women school principals—New York (State)—New York—Biography.   I. Title.
[LD7501.N5M65   1999]
373. 747'1—dc21
99-19298
CIP

First PublicAffairs Edition 1999

30 29 28 27 26 25 24

I am both pleased and flattered that the first edition of *Nothing's Impossible* was so well received by readers from many walks of life. Not only educators, but also business people, health professionals, former students, and government employees have told me how inspirational and useful they found my life's experiences and the lessons of the Monroe Doctrine.

After the 1997 publication of *Nothing's Impossible* and the graduation of the first class of the Frederick Douglas Academy (96% of whom were accepted to college), I founded the School Leadership Academy (SLA) in order to spread the Monroe Doctrine even further. As a new division of the Center for Educational Innovation in New York City, the mission of the SLA is to develop creative, effective "take no prisoners" school leadership. This new work of training principals and public school leaders, which I do both in America and abroad, is a natural outgrowth and continuation of my life's work. The real thrill of the work remains the same: helping others to transform children's lives.

LORRAINE MONROE
January 1999

My thanks to the following people, without whom *Nothing's Impossible* would not have been written:

Peter Osnos, publisher of Public Affairs, who suggested that I write this book;

Dan Cohen of *The New York Times*, who introduced me to Peter Osnos;

Karl Weber, my wise and gentle editor *extraordinaire*;

Mike Hamilburg, my agent, whose unfailing enthusiasm encouraged me;

Kate Darnton, whose patience and expertise moved this edition to publication;

Leonard F. Littwin and Anna E. Lawson, whose examples of leadership were invaluable to my practice and effectiveness.

But first and last, I acknowledge the many blessings I have received from God, that have enabled me to live a life that continues to amaze me and make me grateful every day.

LORRAINE MONROE
New York City
January 1999

CONTENTS

On a Noble Mission

THE FREDERICK DOUGLASS ACADEMY STORY

If you've heard of me, it's probably because of the Frederick Douglass Academy, a special high school in New York's Harlem that I had the privilege of helping to found and run. The academy's success in teaching inner-city kids has won it a lot of attention, including a profile on TV's *60 Minutes*—one of our society's "official" marks of recognition.

As I write these words, in the spring of 1997, the academy is about to graduate its first class of twelfth-graders. About three-quarters of the seniors have already received letters of acceptance to college, and our counselors expect nearly all the rest to be accepted, too. Most of the students haven't yet decided which schools they'll attend, but their acceptances have come from many colleges, including Columbia, Dartmouth, NYU, and the University of Pennsylvania to Temple, Spelman, Morehouse, Colgate, and Smith.

Mind you, this is a *public* high school that draws its students from the Harlem community; the student body is 80 percent African-

American, 20 percent Latino. Admission is selective, as I'll explain later, but the great majority of our students are kids like any others in Harlem. Many come from troubled or broken homes, and most are from families of modest means—or little means. If anyone still claims that black kids, when properly supported, can't learn and compete with anyone else, the results we've achieved at the academy prove otherwise.

As you'll see, my work at the Frederick Douglass Academy was really the culmination of a lifetime of preparation—professional, intellectual, psychological, and spiritual. And now, in addition to consulting with school systems around the United States and the world, I'm deeply involved in an exciting new project, working to start and direct a School Leadership Academy to spread good ideas and methods about running schools in New York's educational system. So the academy has been both a very fulfilling opportunity for me to put into practice all the notions I'd developed about schools, kids, and leadership, and a springboard for new opportunities for the next phase of my life.

A Special School

Like most wonderful things in my life, the chance to run the academy came to me out of a "by the way" conversation. After many years in teaching, a stint as principal at Taft High School in the Bronx, and another as deputy chancellor of New York's Board of Education—the infamous 110 Livingston Street, home of the fabled education bureaucracy of the world's biggest school system—I had been working at a variety of activities, including consulting in schools in Central Harlem. One day in 1990, I was talking to Dr. Bertrand Brown, the superintendent of School District 5, which covers most of Harlem, where many of New York's—and the nation's—most troubled schools can be found. As I was leaving his office, he casually said, "By the way, Lorraine, I've been thinking about opening a special school in the district to prepare kids for college and careers."

Turning from the door and facing him, I responded, "I wouldn't mind being principal of such a school."

"Are you kidding?" he asked. I guess he couldn't believe I would give up the good life of a consultant and professor at Bank Street College of Education for the principalship of a new school in an impoverished, crime-ridden community. And I must admit I loved being a consultant: flying around the world to speak to teachers and principals of schools from Sweden to Japan, being met at airports by blue-jacketed chauffeurs with signs reading "Dr. L. Monroe," riding in limousines, and being put up in good hotels with elegant room service.

But consulting, I'd found, had made me "school-hungry." I missed kids. I missed the smell of books, chalk, and school lunches. I missed the camaraderie of dedicated colleagues, and most of all, I missed the challenge of leadership. I'd been a principal before. I'd been rather good at it. And leadership is addictive: once you've experienced the power to suggest changes and see them happen, you want more of it.

The immediacy of responsibility also called to me, especially when some aspects of consulting became frustrating. Some of the principals that I tried to help by teaching them the simplest empowering tasks and techniques—things like keeping a date book, setting priorities of putting kids before paperwork, and being visible daily—seemed to find these concepts monumentally difficult to put into practice. Since I was just a consultant, there wasn't much I could about it. So I wanted to give the work of principal one more shot.

Finally, I was excited about the idea for a special school in Harlem, a school dedicated to real educational excellence. It wasn't a new idea. Four years earlier, Dr. Brown had told me that he had been trying to convince the school board of the need for a special high school in that part of Harlem. Over time, he had been meeting with less and less resistance, and by 1991 he had almost all the board votes he needed to push through the notion of what had now been identified as the Frederick Douglass Academy. At that time I was consulting and teaching at the Bank Street College of Education in New York.

"Frederick Douglass Can Be!"

Finally, one evening in mid-May of 1991, I heard on my answering machine a message from an exuberant Linda Tarry, a colleague of mine who was head of the Resource and Development team of District 5 and a supporter of the concept from the beginning. "It's a go, it's a go, it's a go!" she shouted. "They voted for the school! Girlfriend, Frederick Douglass can be!"

I was really excited. Here was a chance not just to lead but to *create* a school, putting into it all I had ever done right and all the good ideas I'd read about and heard about in my consulting travels here and abroad. I called Dr. Brown the next day, and he confirmed Linda's message. We made an appointment to meet at a law office on Lexington Avenue. When I got there, I found a team of supporters waiting for me. It included Dr. Brown and Linda Tarry; Joe Cohen, a partner in the law firm of Morrison, Cohen, Singer, and Weinstein; Rick Calvillo, CEO of the public relations firm of Calvillo and Ferrell; Colman Genn, a former principal, superintendent of School District 27 in Queens, and a senior fellow at the Center for Educational Innovation; and Seymour (Sy) Fliegel, also a senior fellow at CEI and author of the book *Miracle in East Harlem.*

"We are here to support you in whatever way we can," they said. I felt overwhelmed and grateful for their faith in me. These early allies gave us important practical help in many ways. Calvillo and Ferrell, for example, provided funds for brochures, supplies, and other necessities during our first two years, and CEI gave us a grant of $15,000 that enabled us to fund the faculty retreat at which we hatched many of our initial plans—as you'll see.

Dr. Brown then asked, "Do you want a year to plan the school, Lorraine?"

I quickly replied, "No, because I've been planning it my whole life. Let's open it this September."

"Here's a concept paper I've drafted," said Dr. Brown. "Work it over so that it includes what you want." He added, "Let's make an appointment to see the school building."

A Subway in the Basement

I n a few days, several of us met at 9:00 a.m. outside the school building. The Frederick Douglass Academy, then known as Intermediate School 10, is located at 149th Street and Adam Clayton Powell Boulevard (once called Seventh Avenue). It was a deeply troubled school—ridden with violence, chaos, low achievement. Our task would be to create a whole new school in the shell of the old, failed institution. We'd use the old building and keep some of the staff, but otherwise we were starting with a clean slate.

The custodian, Al Frey, met us at the door with his assistant, Clark Bullard. "Hi, I'm going to be the new principal," I said. Dr. Brown said, "We're just going to tour around." And we did.

What we saw was daunting. There were burnt bulletin boards in the halls, a burned-out science room, broken ceiling tiles everywhere, a water-damaged music room, new-looking auditorium curtains already badly torn, and a grand piano with missing keys, and bubble gum and pencils stuck in its strings. We ended our tour in the principal's office. The walls were a nondescript color, and the adjacent conference room was festooned with about a hundred paper snowflakes hanging from the light fixtures by strands of sewing thread. The effect resembled clouds of spiderwebs.

"Is it possible to repair these rooms?" I asked Al Frey. He looked non-committal, but asked, "What color do you like?"

"Yellow," I said. "It catches the light of the sun."

As we were leaving, Rick Calvillo said, "This place is a disgrace. How in God's name can kids learn in a place like this? Do you want the *New*

York Times in here? I think I can get them here if you want. Maybe a story about these terrible conditions would wake some people up."

I said, "No, don't call the *Times*. Let them come later, when it's different." (And they did.)

I stopped by the next day to see Al Frey. When I arrived, he said, "I've called around to my custodian friends, and the word is you're okay." He reached in his back pocket and handed me a paint color chart. "Tell me which yellow you like," he said. After I'd picked a shade, he said, "Now, come on—I want to show you what this school sits on."

We went down a flight and a half of stairs and found ourselves not in a cellar but in a cavernous branch of the New York City subway system; there were tracks with trains rumbling to and fro. Al explained, "They built this school over the terminal of the subway train, so we have no basement." To my dismay, I realized there was also no land, no open space in which to plant trees or flowers. And I'd already seen that the school had no lobby—the main entrance was under the stairs to the second floor. I thought, "What engineer had designed this building? And who at the Board of Education had approved the design? Did the fact that the school was located in Harlem make the design unimportant?" I didn't know, but my guess is it was a factor. I could only shake my head in disgust.

We returned to my first-floor office, where I began to work. I shifted my desk closer to the window, facing the morning and afternoon sun, and dragged broken and superfluous furniture into the hall. I filled twenty large trash bags with ancient memos, handouts, and books, unearthing thousands of photos and yearbooks from decades past. I spent two days setting up my personal spaces. Once I got through with it, the setup wasn't bad. I relished having a private bathroom right off my office; at Taft, my first high school, the bathroom was way down the hall, leaving me vulnerable on any trip to the rest room to the inevitable person who would say, "Can I talk to you? This will only take a minute" or "Have you got a second?"

After the mid-May announcement that okayed the academy, I had to recruit new staff. Upon the advice of Dr. Brown and the president of the school board, Mrs. Wynola Glenn, I kept Howard Lew as our assistant principal. With Howard's help, I identified several more teachers, counselors, and other staff members who'd been doing a good job at the old I.S. 10 and who had a contribution to make to our new enterprise. These we retained. The rest of the staff of the Frederick Douglass Academy was new. It was necessary, I felt, to make a clean break from the history of I.S. 10.

Once the word about Frederick Douglass began to spread, my existing reputation and contacts made it easy for me to recruit great teachers. For example, Susan Hui Rohan was a fine math teacher I had mentored for two years at a junior high school on Houston Street in lower Manhattan. She wrote me a letter asking to join our staff, and I was pleased to have her. Lettie Hartwell (science) and Richard Dillon (social studies) were members of a lunchtime group I mentored at another local junior high. They, too, sought jobs at Frederick Douglass. Karole Turner-Stevens was a forceful teacher/administrator at the same school. One afternoon that spring as I was leaving my lunchtime seminar, Karole rushed up to me, fixed me with a stare, and said, "I will be there!"

"What do you mean?" I sputtered, a bit taken aback by the announcement.

"You know what I mean!" Karole replied. "I've heard about your new school—it's all over Harlem. And I will be there!"

Sure enough, I hired Karole, and she in turn recommended other good teachers who ultimately became part of our team.

Mission: Return to Glory

While staff was being interviewed and recruited, I also had to beat the bushes for 150 kids to start our school with. In retrospect, I could and should have started with 75 or 100 kids, but the concept paper that we used as our guiding document said 150, so 150 it was.

As a public school, Frederick Douglass naturally does not charge admission or tuition fees, but we are able to be somewhat selective in the students we admit; since District 5 is a choice district, students have six other middle schools to which they can apply. Although today we can be fairly choosy in finding motivated students who we think will benefit from our program, our admissions counselor chooses a balanced incoming class of students at, above, and below grade level in reading and math. Seventy-five percent of the incoming class must come from Central Harlem; 25 percent can come from anywhere else. The anywhere elses are Brooklyn and the Bronx.

But that first year, 1991, it was very tough sledding to find 150 kids. By mid-May, when the decision was made to launch the school in September, most kids, especially the "desirable" ones for whom school is important, have already chosen their intermediate school. So I had my work cut out for me in recruiting students.

I trotted to every "feeder" school (that is, the elementary schools in our district, whose students would be eligible for the academy), talked to every counselor, spoke at student assemblies, and addressed groups of parents. My primary mission was to convince them that the old I.S. 10 they knew and avoided was closed, finished, and that the Frederick Douglass Academy would be different.

I told them about the wonderful history behind the Frederick Douglass name. Back in the 1920s, '30s, and '40s, there had been a Frederick Douglass school in Harlem (also known as Junior High School 139), which, like our new school, had been a public school with a proud tradition of excellence. The old Frederick Douglass boasted such graduates as Dr. Kenneth Clark, the renowned educator; the great novelist and essayist James Baldwin; Congressman Charles Rangel, still a force in New York and national politics; Olympic runner John Carlos; noted painters Romare Beardon and Jacob Lawrence; actor Brock Peters; filmmaker William Greaves; and theatrical producer/director Voza Rivera, to name but a few. The new Frederick Douglass Academy, I promised, would hark back to these glory days of academic excellence.

Very few parents, kids, counselors, or principals believed me. They remembered only the violence, the out-of-control, no-learning atmosphere of the old I.S. 10. Some knew of my reputation as the principal who had turned around Taft in the Bronx, but most didn't care. As far as most parents were concerned, there was no way they were going to let their precious, smart, well-behaved, college-bound child attend I.S. 10—even if it was now the Frederick Douglass Academy.

So Martha Brown, the district's director of guidance, and I pored over the few applications we received, looking desperately for 150 kids we could enroll. They came from a few brave parents who were willing to take a chance on this new idea, new transfers to the district (who maybe didn't know what they were getting themselves into), and a collection of left-over kids who had scored in the 15th, 20th, and 30th percentiles on their reading and math exams. Frankly, at that time I wasn't sure exactly what the implications of the percentiles were, until Martha Brown, who was eager to place these kids, told me simply that scoring in the 15th percentile allowed students to move on to the next grade. This was hardly the cream of the crop.

It wasn't easy, but we met our quota of 150 students. We picked 50 percent boys and 50 percent girls, and as we placed them in classes we tried to balance out as much as possible boys and girls. In this haphazard way, we achieved a degree of heterogeneity.

Leadership, the Essential Ingredient

How does one go about creating a school like the Frederick Douglass Academy? It's a question I'm asked all the time, especially in these days of declining confidence in our school systems and a growing urgency on the part of educators, parents, and community leaders to try something new that will work for our kids. There's no easy recipe, but here's the formula we followed.

First and foremost, get a leader who is fearless (or perhaps crazy) enough to take well-calculated risks. Fearless enough to enjoy taking a leap into the void. Fearless in that she is not afraid of getting canned. (I'd had that happen once, to my surprise and chagrin, and ultimately found that it led to my elevation into another lovely, challenging destiny. Never again would I fear being fired.) Fearless because, more times than not, smart risks are worth the gamble and they work.

Seek, too, a leader who aspires to a *noble* ideal of education. Noble because this work of transforming children's lives is particularly ennobling. Noble because the work has merit only when done for no reason except to transform children's lives. Noble because the work is necessary work in the highest sense of *mission*—what one *is sent to do* for others. Look for someone who is willing to test every decision against this highest standard of transformational leadership.

It doesn't hurt to have a record of excellent performance in the résumé of the leader. He or she should be a person who loved an academic subject and taught it well. She may even be a person whose aspirations never included leadership outside the classroom. (That was certainly the case with me, until the "leadership bug" bit me after many years of teaching.)

And once you've identified the leader who will spearhead your new creation, surround him or her with a group of insanely dedicated followers, a few people who can infect the rest of the staff with the values and ideals that make education or any work exciting, fruitful, and worthwhile.

I was lucky enough to begin with a group of maniac teachers, counselors, paraprofessionals, aides, and security officers who believed that the former splendor of Frederick Douglass could be again. Let me list their names. As they already know, I can never thank them too much.

Howard Lew, assistant principal
Susan Hui Rohan, mathematics
Richard Dillon, social studies

Isadore Mazliah, carpentry
Andrew Garner, English
Cathleen Tierney, English
Gladys Hill, reading
Lettie Hartwell, science
Pascale Jean-Louis, French
David Simon, computer
Marian Carew, library
Marc Austen, art
Karole Turner-Stevens, Whole Life Management
Edna Hayes, special counselor
Robert Archer, counselor
Rosa Williams, bilingual paraprofessional
Esteban Guijarro, bilingual paraprofessional
Dorothy Jackson, aide
Laura Gadson, physical education (dance)
Ted Smith, physical education
Lynda Reeves, security officer
Robert Watson, security officer
Isabel Mieli, secretary
Denise Corley, secretary

Some of these core staff were already there, at the old I.S. 10, waiting for me; others were drawn specifically by the promise of our new enterprise. For the leader, it's not a matter of being able to handpick your staff. If you know how to find, support, and inspire them, I think that every organization contains dedicated people who are willing to work hard on behalf of change. In all schools, there is a core of teachers waiting to be inspired, galvanized, led, and let go to work their dreams. When I became principal of Taft High School, I could not select my staff—the only change the school board made in the effort to rescue that failing school was to bring in a new leader. I found, contrary to

what most people think, that a leader who seeks out the positive maver-
icks, the creatively crazy people in an existing organization, and supports them while observing, assisting, and developing other staff can
begin to turn an organization around.

So in the end, the apparent quality of the staff isn't the crucial element in building a great school. Leadership is. The ability to choose staff
when starting a new school just makes the excellence happen faster.

I've seen this principle operating in several places. When I was a kid
in Harlem, I attended P.S. 157 on 126th Street and St. Nicholas Avenue.
The principal at that time was a shadow person, a woman who mostly
remained in her office, unseen and unknown. The school's real leader,
though unofficial and I'm sure underpaid, was James Cooper—a tall,
handsome, imperial, well-dressed African-American man. He ran
everything—assemblies, guest speakers, appearances of the gospel
choir, and the student government. He was wonderfully warm and
strict, a benevolent terrorist. I learned many things from Mr. Cooper:
that structure was a fine and helpful thing; that African-Americans have
always contributed to American society; that gospel music can save
your soul; that Robert's Rules of Order govern meetings; and that setting high expectations and teaching kids to reach them is the job of any
educator. But above all I learned from him the importance of the
leader—the visibility, mobility, and inspiration of the leader—in making any organization work. That's the key lesson, I think, for anyone
who wants to start a school that can do what the Frederick Douglass
Academy does.

Dreams of Difference

In building the academy, my initial tactic was to take all that I had
learned as a kid in school, as a teacher in four schools, as a principal,
as a school administrator, as a professor, and as an international consul-

tant and put it all to work in one place. It was an unlikely place—a failing Central Harlem school located in a neighborhood diverse in income, ethnicity (African-American, Latinos, East Indians), and housing: a neighborhood of co-ops, empty lots, tenement apartments, abandoned buildings, crack houses, and Harlem Renaissance town houses.

In this setting, our goal was to create a school concerned with excellence, quality, and equity, one that would train kids to be competitors at the highest level. I knew that the quality we sought would be based not on our location or on the ethnic and social makeup of the neighborhood but on the high level of expectations and beliefs of the person in the front of each classroom and on the vision, acts, energy, and courage of the person in the principal's chair.

Beginning with my second year of teaching, I'd begun to have a sense of what was not working in school, especially why so many kids were unruly and not learning. It was then that I began to realize that school leadership was the key in determining whether a school was successful or a killer of children. I began to connect with like-minded colleagues. We would sit in the teachers' lounge, analyze the stupid administrative moves we observed, and spin dreams of difference for us and the kids we taught. Some of us used to talk about buying a brownstone and starting our own school, where we'd "do school right."

Unfortunately, we never moved past talking. When I think of the power of the crazy, creative maniacs who actually carried that first school where I taught and what a great school we could have created, I regret our timidity and lack of daring in not starting our own school. Somewhere in the years that followed, I lost the vision of creating a school of my own. Not until I was offered the chance to open the Frederick Douglass Academy did those long-ago thoughts come to the front of my consciousness. Opening Frederick Douglass Academy, I thought, is about the closest I'd ever come to creating the school that my colleagues and I had dreamed about decades ago.

Once the go-ahead was given in May, I started committing my dreams to 8½-by–11-inch yellow pads with a number 2 pencil. First, I decided that I wanted our kids to wear uniforms—to eliminate competition about the externals and concerns about who has what and to get the kids to focus on what was going on in their heads as opposed to what was on their backs. Uniforms are cheaper than a wardrobe of outfits, and they look good, too. I believe that uniforms matter, since kids tend to behave the way they're dressed.

I also decided that we would have a closed-campus, or "captive," lunch—that is, no leaving school in the middle of the day. Previously I had seen kids from I.S. 10 using their free student transit passes to ride long distances on subway trains and buses to fast-food restaurants, often returning 30 to 60 minutes late for their afternoon classes. No more!

I wanted to offer our students an academically rigorous college-preparation program to train them for competition beyond what they'd find in the local high schools, just as kids in suburban schools or private prep schools are prepared to compete against the best in the nation for college acceptances.

At the same time, I wanted to balance the academic rigor with lots of extracurricular club and team activities. When I interviewed potential staff members, I asked, "What two other things can you offer kids other than your subject?" This was a totally illegal question: the terms of the contract between the teachers' union and the Board of Education forbid requiring teachers to perform any extra service for which they do not receive pay. But no one I interviewed objected. They understood that lots of kids come to school mainly because of a club or team they love, and that any extracurricular activity that is taught well gives kids success skills and competencies that can translate into academic success, provided that the *transference* of qualities like discipline, perseverance, and patience is discussed and demonstrated by the club or team advisor. We also know that kids who get to know teachers in informal club or team relationships are less likely to vandalize, get into trouble, or cut school.

Although we opened our doors with a very small staff, thanks to the talents and generosity of our teachers, we started with clubs for dance, basketball, volleyball, dominoes, track, art, French, computers, and science, and we've added to the list subsequently. By our third year, we offered a total of thirty-two clubs and activities.

Starting with a Plan

Once the initial staff was chosen, the Manhattan Institute, through its Center for Educational Innovation, gave us a grant that allowed us to have a staff retreat at a conference center in Tarrytown, New York. This retreat enabled us to sit and dream the school for which all of us had so long yearned:

❑ a place where teaching and learning were honored and taken seriously

❑ a place of order and predictability

❑ a place where kids, especially boys, could learn that it was okay to be smart

❑ a place where teachers would have a great deal of autonomy in choosing texts, materials, and methodology—as long as the methodology worked

We gathered at the conference center on the last Thursday before Labor Day and met to discuss what we wanted in our school. Order was our first priority, and together we made up our list of twelve non-negotiable rules and regulations. They have not changed over the years, except that after three years we added the section describing the consequences for violating the principles, which we had always observed anyway (see page 17).

FREDERICK DOUGLASS ACADEMY

Preface to the Twelve Non-Negotiable Rules and Regulations:

RESPECT YOURSELF:
Do only those things that will help you to achieve a successful and healthful future.

RESPECT YOUR ASSOCIATES:
Treat your associates with courtesy, justice and truthfulness.

RESPECT PROPERTY:
Take care of your things and take care of those things which we share.

The Twelve Non-Negotiable Rules and Regulations:

1. Attend school daily and come on time. There is late detention.
2. Leave all outer clothing in your classroom closet.
3. Move quickly from class to class. Enter the room quietly, take your assigned seat, and begin work immediately.
4. Be prepared to work every day. Bring large looseleaf notebook, assignment notebook, pens, pencils, rulers, protractors, and whatever equipment is required for learning.
5. Do homework nightly. There is homework detention and homework help.
6. Eat only in the cafeteria. Gum chewing and candy are prohibited even in the cafeteria.
7. Do not bring radios, walkmen, beepers, or games to school.
8. Keep your desk area clean.
9. Do not engage in physical or verbal violence. Learn to disagree without being disagreeable. Do not fight.

10. Respect the building. Do not graffiti or deface any part of the building.
11. Show your student program card or ID card to any adult in authority in the building who requests it.
12. Wear the school uniform daily. Hats are not to be worn in the building.

YOUNG WOMEN:
White blouse, navy skirt of decent length and closed-in black shoes. In cold and inclement weather, the school uniform must be worn. Wear navy or white tights. Navy blazers or sweaters. No bathroom changing of clothes allowed. No large jewelry.

YOUNG MEN:
White shirt, navy pants, belt, navy ties and black shoes. Navy blazers or sweaters.

GYM:
Navy shorts, white tee shirt, white sneakers
* No bathroom passes are given during the first 15 or the last 10 minutes of a period.

CONSEQUENCES:
1. Conference with involved teacher
2. Conference with counselor
3. Conference with parent
4. In-house suspension
5. Out of the academy
6. Transfer to another school

We also began to plan our school year, mapping out month by month the special occasions, rituals, ceremonies, and activities on which our school's life would be centered. This annual mapping of the year has become an academy tradition. For example:

SEPTEMBER
  Orientation
  Diagnostic tests
  First Parents' Association meeting
  Course outlines distributed to parents
  First big in-school exams
  Spring exam preparation beings

OCTOBER
  First report card
  Extracurricular activities begin

NOVEMBER
  Open School day and night for parents
  Gala performance—a show highlighting each academic department
    through song, dance, or recitation
  Penny Harvest—a citywide school project created by the nonprofit group
    Common Cents, to collect pennies to help feed the homeless
  Food baskets—collection of canned and dried foods for the poor

DECEMBER
  Celebration of Light—a ceremony featuring the significance of light in
    the holidays of Christmas, Hanukkah, and Kwanzaa
  Toy drive for children at Harlem Hospital and North General Hospital
  Christmas-break assignment

JANUARY
  Reorientation assemblies
  Midyear exams

FEBRUARY
  Black History Month
  Intensive exam preparation
  Midwinter break assignment

MARCH

Women's program—performances at school assemblies and special discussion of women's contributions in subject classes

APRIL

Spring-break assignment

MAY

Dance and drama—evening performances (fundraisers)

JUNE

Field Day

Final exams and New York State Regents exams

Awards assembly

Eighth-grade graduation

Faculty party

On our retreat, we also spent a great deal of time nailing down Day One. What exactly would we do on the first day of school? What did we want the kids to do? We were so anxious for it to be perfect that, after the staff returned from the Labor Day vacation on the day before school would open, we walked through a Day One dress rehearsal. In doing so, we found glitches, which we ironed out without the chaos of 150 kids experiencing the glitches. For example, we walked into the cafeteria just as the kids would do, to find a series of tables labeled alphabetically according to kids' last names (A–K, L–M, and so on), where they'd get their homeroom designations. When we did this, we realized that the kids would have to sit and be called so that the tables wouldn't be swamped. We also discovered which letters of the alphabet had the heaviest traffic and changed A–K to A–E accordingly. We gave each teacher a stiff pennant with his or her homeroom printed on it so the kids could easily find their homeroom teachers in the auditorium.

We instituted a philosophy of Day One seriousness to set a tone of learning and order from the very beginning. Routines would be explained with a logical rationale for each, and homework would be given. Some of this would happen during an extended homeroom and some during the regular classes, which the students attended during the day. Every teacher would be obligated to go over the twelve Non-Negotiables in class, so that by 2:15 all children would have heard them at least four times.

At 2:15, the entire school, 150 kids, would come to the auditorium to be greeted by me, the other administrators, the counselors, and the other teachers. For the last time that day they would hear the twelve Non-Negotiables, this time from me. If you want something to sink in, don't say it once! Say it over and over! I call this the Rule of Saturation or Pervasiveness of Expectations. It's part of my leadership method, which I've dubbed The Monroe Doctrine. (You'll hear more about it throughout the book.)

To Advance, Retreat!

Back to the planning retreat. After mapping out our procedures for Day One, we worked out a Week One calendar, which was an expansion of the Day One with the addition of teachers laying out the work for the semester and/or the year and giving diagnostic tests. The results of these tests would be used to revise teacher plans to better meet our particular kids' needs. The essential things to establish during Week One would be that summer is over, this is a serious place, you will work hard, but you will love it because we've planned wonderful things for you to do.

On the first day of the retreat, we worked from 8:30 to noon, lunched from noon till 1:15, and then worked till 4:00. Then we had free time to swim, play Ping-Pong or tennis, or use the workout room. Then we enjoyed a long, leisurely dinner, followed by some of us going to our rooms, others bowling or sitting around laughing and talking, and still others finding a place to dance. (I tried to do all of these.) The next day, we were back at work from 8:30 till noon, followed by a great lunch, and then we were off for the Labor Day weekend. We left ready to start the new school year with enthusiasm, so emotionally and mentally high that we almost wished school was the next day.

We have continued these retreats, supported by corporate funding, every year for six years, and their importance can't be overestimated. Each year, staff is able to get away from school to reflect on the past year: What was planned? What was accomplished? What needs to be scrapped? What needs to be altered? What needs to remain the same? This internal examination is beneficial to our growth as an institution and to our professional growth as individuals. The retreat also incorporates new staff into the culture of the school and into the social milieu as we eat, joke, play, and dance together. Finally, it allows me to address the staff away from the school to remind them of our mission, our past accomplishments, and where we need to be headed in the coming year.

While it is quite possible to do all of this on site at the school, the distractions of familiar turf would be a real problem. You know the sort of thing I mean: "I just want to run up to my room for a minute" or "Let me get some stuff out of my car—it'll only take a sec." When these are eliminated, total focus can be trained on the business at hand, which is predicated on a well-thought-out, tightly planned agenda.

In my mind, except for meals and the Thursday-evening dancing, the retreat means hard work, hard thinking, and an ironclad commitment to setting up a September–June calendar that will be a guide to enable us to run the school smoothly. I use my Thursday-morning address as a bully pulpit, where I remind the whole team of the overarching reason for our being. I am always consciously *corny*, and, I hope, inspiring, calling forth everyone's best instincts for doing the work.

Day One Arrives

The day before the kids came back, the day after Labor Day, the school was alive with activity. Al Frey and his men had worked through the summer to repair the damage we'd seen on our first, disheartening visit, and they had the building sparkling: everything was freshly painted yellow and blue, the floors were buffed so that the light bounced off them, and the gym floor looked ready for ballroom dancing. Thelma Owens, the "bulletin board queen," had put fresh backing on every bulletin board. Every teacher was busy arranging chairs into his or her preferred configuration: circles, squares, U's, quads, pairs, or old-fashioned straight rows. Some put their own desks square in the middle, some on the side, and some in the back in a corner. "Welcome" and the teacher's name and homeroom class were written on the board. Plan books already had Day One and Week One entries. They were ready.

I was ready, too. I had put up my Welcome Back to School sign, filled my bulletin board with a collection of favorite postcards, put up my poster from the Broadway show *For Colored Girls . . .*, and taped a small poster of Vincent van Gogh on the inside of my closet door. I positioned on my windowsill two plants: the snake plant my mother gave me for luck when I went off to teach my first day at Junior High School 81 (West 120th Street), and the plant I'd found in the street when my husband and I were courting, in the sixties. (Both plants have gone with me to every new place I've worked, and both are still alive after all these years! A good omen, surely.) In the corner of the windowsill, I placed a picture of St. George slaying the dragon that a kid had given me when I was girls' dean at Adlai E. Stevenson High School in the Bronx—a metaphor for the work I do. Yes, I was ready.

It was a bright, sunny, warm September day when the new Frederick Douglass Academy opened its doors to our first 150 kids. Although we had casually considered that maybe the staff should wear navy and white, like the kids, the idea wasn't really pursued; but on that first morning, *everyone* had on navy and white. The doors were officially opened at 8:00—classes would start at 8:45—but kids and their parents began arriving soon after 7:00. Some parents had driven up onto the terrace and were standing near their cars watching as their kids shyly moved away to greet old friends that had been accepted into the academy. Several of us were on the terrace to greet the kids and their parents. The sun seemed a beneficent presence, blessing our first day.

At 8:00, we asked the children to enter and told the parents that their children would be dismissed at 2:50. In order to keep the traffic flowing, we told parents to remain outside. I don't know how it happened, but one mother got past the security guard and up to the door of the cafeteria where the children were assembling. She looked in and saw—as I did, simultaneously—the sea of blinding white shirts and blouses on children waiting in an orderly fashion for the next set of instructions. She stepped back, threw up her arms, jumped into the air, and shouted, "Hallelujah, praise God—school how it ought to be!"

I thought, "Amen to that."

Day One went smoothly as we had planned. When they weren't in the classroom, the teachers were walking around with broad smiles on their faces. After the welcome and orientation assembly at the end of the day, I stood by the door at dismissal and watched the kids leaving. I heard one kid say to another, "This is a *do-now school*! But I think I'm going to like it."

"We're Number One!"

Week One flowed smoothly, then Month One and Month Two slipped by. The plans we'd carefully laid out in August were working. Sooner than I imagined, December was upon us, and one day in a flash I realized that in a few months—in April, to be exact—our kids would be taking their city and state exams. These were a crucial measure of how the Frederick Douglass Academy was performing. Each school's scores and standings were published in the *New York Times* every year, and I.S. 10, from whose ashes we'd risen, was always at or near the bottom of the 179 middle schools in the city of New York. If this year the scores were strong, they would say to the world, "The Frederick Douglass Academy is indeed an effective school."

Having done my rounds daily and having observed each teacher for at least one full period—I'm a great believer in being everywhere, seeing and being seen, as a vital leadership tool—I knew that good teaching was going on. But I knew also that in the community there was some jealousy and animosity directed against the academy. Our success would throw into sharp contrast what was *not* happening in the other schools, raising uncomfortable questions. So while some people were rooting for us to succeed, others quietly hoped for our academic downfall.

I knew how to prepare kids to ace exams—I'd done it ever since I'd begun teaching. As I pondered our progress that December morning, I thought to myself, "Maybe we'd better identify those kids who are likely not to get through the tests in reading and math." If middle-class kids could be trained and tutored, so could our kids; if our parents could not afford tutoring at private centers like Kaplan, we'd do it in-house. I sketched out a battle plan, then sent out a call for tutors via my weekly staff bulletin: "If you are willing to tutor in reading and/or math, please come to lunch on Wednesday in my conference room."

Seven teachers showed up. I gave them a list of seventy students, targeted by the faculty as students who might be in danger of failing the exams, and each chose ten kids. We decided to have tutoring sessions at 7:45 a.m., at lunchtime, and at 3:00 p.m.—teachers would choose time slots convenient to them. Letters were sent to the parents saying, "At his/her present level of skills, your child will not pass the reading test. We have set up tutoring sessions to help him/her. Attendance is not optional. Your child must attend. Please sign below that you have read this and that you are willing to let your child attend these sessions. This tear-off should be brought to your child's first session."

We made further plans. We all agreed that a diagnostic test was important to set individual improvement plans. We all agreed that test language, test analysis, and test timing skills should be taught and that mock tests should be given periodically to assess progress. This system began in January after the midyear exams and continued until the April and May exams. Nearly all the targeted students participated as required, helped along by the fact that our teachers would visit the cafeteria to find and hound any laggards, and personally escort some reluctant kids to their sessions.

One day in mid-May, Mr. Lew, our assistant principal, went to the district office to pick up the academy's test results. Gladys Hill, the reading teacher, sat in the general office near mine, waiting quietly though somewhat anxiously for Mr. Lew's return. When he walked into the office, he was expressionless. Ms. Hill got up, and I came out of my office.

"So, Lew," I asked, "what's it look like?"

"Well," he said, "we're number one in the district and number eleven in all of New York City."

Ms. Hill beamed and tears began to roll down her cheeks. I let out a yell. "Number one in the district! Number eleven in New York City! Wait till next year, Gladys," I said, giving her a congratulatory hug. "Wait till next year—we've only been practicing!"

We waited till 3 o'clock to tell the staff and kids over the loudspeaker, because I anticipated that they'd be loud in their joy. I was right. When they were dismissed at the door, many twirled and leaped, yelling, "We're number one! We're number one!" Their joy was mingled with disbelief. So many of them had come from failing schools with histories of low expectations. Their pride in their triumph over the tests that had so long bested so many of them made their loud celebration legitimate.

Much the same could be said about the teachers' reactions to the results that their hard work had produced. I'd known it was possible. Now they all knew it, and there was no turning back.

We continued our tutorial tradition for the next five years, varying it only slightly. We now have a four-step program:

1. Identify kids who are in danger of failing in September;

2. begin exam preparation immediately, using teacher-made exam questions that mirror the questions on the standardized exams;

3. include all subjects that terminate in standardized city or state exams in this tutorial system; and

4. give mock exams in the cafeteria under conditions that mirror the "big test day."
   This system has worked well for our students with every subject except biology and chemistry. This problem is being seriously looked at and worked on during the current school year.

This system has worked well for our students with every subject except biology and chemistry. This problem is being seriously looked at and worked on during the current school year.

"We Expect You to Be Special"

Ending our first year with these well-publicized successes in math and reading made a big difference in how our kids viewed themselves. When they went out on trips—for example, to the Metropolitan Museum of Art to look at and sketch the wonderful artworks—they were often asked by passersby, "What private school is this?"

"No," they now replied with undisguised pride. "This is a public school—the Frederick Douglass Academy!" (By the way, am I glad I chose to use the word *academy* in our name, as opposed to *school, high school,* or *institute. Academy* has a ring to it and gives the school cachet.)

Staff morale got a boost, too. Teachers now realized for certain that the academy was a good place to teach. Even more important, we began to get the reputation in the Harlem community of being an up-and-coming school. With even better test scores the second year, we were still number one in the district and moved up to number seven in New York City. We continued to enroll 150 seventh-graders each September, but whereas before we opened, I'd had to beg counselors and parents to trust me and to believe in the future of the school enough to send me their kids, I now had to turn away applicants.

Now whenever a kid wasn't accepted, I would get irate phone calls from politicians, board members, and parents. It became extremely important for the counselor who screened our incoming kids to select a broad intellectual spectrum of students into the academy, especially since, even before the end of our second year, we were being accused of "creaming Harlem" to achieve our fine results. Most often, these complaints weren't addressed to me personally, but when I had an opportunity to respond, I'd say, "Harlem is in bad shape if it can produce *only* 150 gifted kids."

The fact is that we tell our kids, "You have been specially chosen to attend this special school, and we expect you to be special in every way." The kids believe us, and we then proceed to *make* them gifted and talented—the job of *any* school worth its salt.

Picking Winners, Growing Winners

Thanks to Pascale Jean-Louis, our talented math teacher, we had seventeen *seventh*-graders take the *ninth*-grade New York State Regents exam in algebra. Fifteen passed; one boy scored 100 percent, and several scored in the high 90s. The two who didn't pass (with grades in the 60s) had failed to come to tutorial, choosing instead to go to cheerleading practice. I spoke to them regarding priorities, and they passed at the end of the next semester.

All our seventh-graders—our largest incoming group each year—take English, reading, math (pre-algebra or algebra), social studies, science, French, art, physical education, computers, and Whole Life Management. This last course is one mandated by the state; its proper name is Home and Career Skills. Since I found this a little ambiguous and the curriculum hazy, I renamed it Whole Life Management and gave the class to Karole Turner-Stevens, a wonderfully charismatic teacher with a theatrical background. Between us, we decided that the focus of the course would be to help our seventh-graders develop skills that would enable them to succeed in school and life: organizing their time, their notebooks, and their money; making good choices of companions; knowing how to study effectively and speak effectively; knowing how to order nutritious food at a fast-food restaurant. We've just heard that our Whole Life Management curriculum may become a citywide program in the near future.

We offered French after recruiting Pascale Jean-Louis, a talented Haitian teacher trained in math, who taught the course with the promise that I would seriously hunt for a French teacher for next year and that when I found him or her, she could teach math forever. She was good, and in the course of a year I found Ira Simmonds, a spectacular French teacher and a spectacular person. Managing with this spirit of autonomy and flexibility—with accountability—allows us to use people's talents well for the benefit of our kids.

Each year as we added new staff for the new seventh-graders, the teacher-screening committee and I tried to pick winners: people who would fit the culture of creatively crazy workaholics; people who came early and stayed late; people who talked constantly about individual kids, programs, and projects; people for whom interdisciplinary cooperation is a natural part of professional behavior; people for whom a monthly 3 o'clock faculty conference usually continued with informal conversations and food till 5, 6, or 7 o'clock. Such teachers are not as rare as many people believe; what is rare is the supportive environment that we provide for one another, which makes it possible—even fun!—to work this hard.

Did we make any hiring mistakes? Sure. But most of the teachers I regretted hiring either left or improved with monitoring and assistance. Unfortunately, one or two got tenure who didn't deserve it. But for the most part, we picked well or we could not have kept doing well.

Sports and Scholarship

As the Frederick Douglass Academy approached its third year, the rituals and traditions that help to make a school into a community were set. As at any school, sports was an important element. Basketball became a serious sport, and my gym teachers and I tried unsuccessfully to join the Public School Athletic League, as did all the small, new schools in the city. The answer from the Central Board at 110 Livingston Street was no. Lack of money was the reason. High school varsity sports really matter; not only do the kids, teachers, and parents all enjoy them, but they affect college acceptances and scholarships. But supporting sports without funding is terribly difficult. For two years, I found funds to pay referees. My coaches raised money for uniforms—an important symbolic thing, for sure. Few high school kids would consider playing on a school team without uniforms in the school colors.

Still, not having a league to play in rankled. What were our kids supposed to feel except not as good as the older schools? So my coordinator of the Physical Education Department, Zan Taylor, and the coach of the boys' varsity basketball team, Patrick Mangan, set about organizing a league for the new schools. Both our girls' and boys' varsity basketball teams were city champs of the New School Athletic League in 1995. In the fall of 1996, we are finally on the PSAL schedule, but we still have to find our own funds for coaches, referees, and other expenses for almost every sport we participate in. We have no alternative—"If you don't pay, you don't play." It seems unfair, but I can't rob my twelfth-graders of the opportunity of playing in the "Major Leagues" against the old establishment teams. I have just discovered that in the fall of 1997 we will be funded by the PSAL.

The best part of all this is that many of the boys and girls on the honor roll are on the varsity and junior varsity basketball teams. Skills carry over and correlate, and perseverance and practice pay off in the classroom as well as on the court. Pat Mangan calls our students who take part in sports "*Scholar*-scholar-athletes." He doubles the word "scholar" to indicate the proper emphasis. In fact, he won't allow an athlete to take part in practice until he or she has put in two hours of study time with him that day.

A Place to Learn, a Place to Live

The academy has continued to expand and develop in other ways, too. After the third year of good academic successes, it was personally important for me to have some new things to work on in order to stay vital and energized. I hate "the same old same old" in my life and my work. We introduced Spanish, Japanese, and then Latin to our curriculum. How exciting! Few schools anywhere, and certainly not in Harlem, offer four foreign languages. We recruited outside supporters who gave us financial help and other types of aid so that the kids could come to school as early as 7:45 in the morning and stay late, till after 5:00 or 6:00. I felt it was essential to make the academy central in our children's lives, since many kids did not have quiet places to study, ready access to tutors and mentors, or community recreation centers in which to play sports or take part in other activities. We offered basketball, soccer, volleyball, tennis, track, homework help in the library, art and computer clubs, French club, and tutoring in every major subject.

The value of these special offerings came home starkly to me many times. One time on Holy Thursday, the Thursday before Easter and our last day of school before spring break, I heard three girls chatting outside my office. I came out to see who they were and said, "Girls, go home! The vacation has begun!"

"I don't want to go home," one said. I waited to hear her laugh and get up to leave. Instead, the other girls agreed. "We don't want to go home. Can we sleep over?"

"Come into my office," I replied. "Put some popcorn in the microwave. You want to play a game? Connect Four? Monopoly? Life?"

They all yelled, "Connect Four!" The girls sat in my office for nearly an hour eating popcorn and laughing and playing. Finally, they cleaned up and left, prepared to face being away from the academy for ten long days.

Another time, the basketball coach arranged for the team and a few cheerleaders to celebrate the end of the season in my conference room with a delivered Chinese dinner and the finals of the NCAA college basketball tournament on cable. The boys and girls tumbled into the room and ate as only bottomless-pit adolescents can. "Dr. Monroe, you got any cards?" one asked.

"I think I have a confiscated deck in my desk drawer."

I gave them the cards. Some played cards among themselves or with teachers; others played Connect Four, Monopoly, and Life. It got to be seven o'clock. "Okay, okay, listen up," I said. "It's time for *Jeopardy*, and I'm a *Jeopardy* fan." So we all watched *Jeopardy* together, yelling out right and wrong answers, laughing when we were wrong and cheering when we were right.

After *Jeopardy* they went right on eating and playing. I sat back and watched the kids being with each other and their teachers. It was a scene out of Sunday afternoon in my own living room. I knew we were on to something. At the next faculty conference, I announced that I would fund any teacher who wanted to have dinner in my conference room with kids he or she advised or coached. Many took me up on this, so I wrote a Dinner Proposal for funding and actually made it a formal tradition at the academy.

Real School: From Dream to Reality

All that these past five years have meant and have taught me is mostly very sweet to recall. Yet to have stimulated and sustained the pursuit of excellence was not as easy as my friends and colleagues seemed to believe, watching me work with high energy and laughter. No, it wasn't easy at all.

That the life of a leader is lonely is a cliché not often understood. Leaders have plenty of company—other leaders, bureaucrats, staff, family, and friends—so lonely in the obvious sense is not what is meant. The loneliness of the leader lies in having to think and dream about the work all day, every day, day after day, and then make what you think and dream understandable, palatable, and workable by those who have not thought and dreamed as deeply or as far into the future as you have.

Most important is that the leader continue not only to believe in the dream and the need to pursue it but also to do the hard brain work of never doubting its importance. Oh, doubts will arise, because of the setbacks and failures that inevitably occur, as well as the intrusive demands of life, time, people, and personal life. But the leader's job is to master those doubts and press on. That is the loneliness that cannot be fully shared with anyone, except God in prayer and contemplation.

Apart from spiritual strength I derived from conversation with God, two things assisted me in overriding doubt during my fourteen years of leadership. One was the wonderful, hardworking assistants and staff I had. The other was the habit I'd developed over time of pursuing my goals with persistence and strength—something impossible to do without "rightness of purpose."

My five-year stint at the academy called forth every bit of forcefulness and thoroughness I possessed. I cultivated the ability not to see problems as problems and to ignore bureaucratic edicts. I practiced delaying implementation of the newest contrived and mandated "solutions" for "at-risk kids" (read *poor children, children of color, children of immigrants*). My years as a teacher have shown me that "new solutions" and bureaucratic edicts invariably miss the mark. To me, the challenge of education is simple:

To teach the children who come, regardless of race, religion, ethnicity, socioeconomic background, or gender, how to read, write, think, com-

pute, appreciate the arts, speak well, and behave in socially acceptable ways, so that they can become economically independent, contributing members of society.

Strange to say, I break into a sweat writing this, because the common sense of this approach seems to elude many people associated with schools and with the development of educational policies, practices, and budgets. How to create what I call *real school* is already known. It exists in pockets of excellence scattered around the world. Our inability or reluctance, caused either by prejudice or lack of training, to create real schools and make them available to all children works cruelly against the success of needy kids. Both inability and reluctance can be addressed over time with planning, training, flexibility, monitoring, cooperation, and equitable funding.

The heart of the matter is that requiring solid, challenging, interesting work on a par with what excellent public and private schools *demand* works, with poor kids and with all kids.

What is good for the best is good for the rest. To do anything less is obscene.

On Working from the Heart

If you don't love the work you're doing, you'll get sick—physically, mentally, or spiritually. Eventually, you'll make others sick, too.

≈

All good work is worthy of our dedication. And the most worthy is what changes lives profoundly—in mind, body, and spirit.

≈

Worthwhile work is rarely done strictly from nine to five.

≈

If you're ambitious, doing your job well is the only way to rise with your dignity and integrity intact—owing no one.

≈

If you're indifferently supervised, do the crazy, unexpected, wonderful thing you've always dreamed of.

≈

Any life can be a work of art. So how can we but work in the belief that we *will* make a difference?

CHAPTER 2

Gifts of the Ancestors

LASTING LEGACIES OF MY EARLY LIFE

We are each shaped by the people who gave us life. Everything we are and all that we do can be traced back, in one way or another, to early influences: parents, family, a home or the lack of a home. In my case, four figures from my childhood helped to make me who I am, each giving me a gift that is unique: my father, my mother, my grandmother, and my grandfather. To understand me, you have to know them.

The Gift of Passion

Are there enough pages in this book to write about the powerful influence of my father on my personal and professional life? When I was little, I thought he was a giant—he seemed so tall, so broad, so strong. He had large hands: callused from hard labor, quick to hit, strong to hold on to, and smooth to dance with. I was afraid of him. But I loved him—really adored him.

Like so many of us, James Edward Williams was a hard-to-understand blend of the wonderful and terrible. Only nineteen when I was born, he remained a boy in many ways through his whole life. He found it hard to control his temper, he could be violent without warning or provocation, and yet he could be the *funnest* person anyone knew. He had a great sense of humor and was great at reading us stories, especially the tales of Uncle Remus. He loved board games. He taught me to leg wrestle, to dance, to catch a softball with a fielder's glove, and to throw overhand "like a boy." And he taught me to walk fast, always: "You gotta walk fast, baby, if you want to keep up with Daddy!"

Much of the joy that I have in living I owe to my dad's teaching. He taught me to spend money, to enjoy people, to laugh a lot. He showed me how to savor food and to relish going out with family or friends. Whenever Dad had to babysit me and my sister Ruthie, he took us to eat at a local restaurant, the Cosmos on 124th Street and St. Nicholas Avenue in Harlem. I thought eating out was *it*. Later I learned why we ate out so often: he couldn't cook, and he wouldn't learn. He tried once when I was six; he fixed soft-boiled eggs. I refused to eat them, because, as I told him, they looked like brains. He threw the egg cup at me, missing my head by just a few inches, but at least I didn't have to eat the "egg brains."

Another food incident happened when I was six. Dad loved sausage, and one day he sent me to the store on the corner of our block at 118th Street and Eighth Avenue to get him some breakfast link pork sausage. I went and ran back. He was in bed when I presented the bag with the sausage to him. He opened it and found Polish sausage.

"What the hell is this?" he cried. "*Polish* sausage! This is not what I sent you for!" I started sniveling.

"I asked you to get pork sausage!" Daddy yelled.

I whimpered, "That's what the man gave me, and he said it was pork sausage."

Daddy hit me two or three times with the sausage and said, "Take it back and get my money back!" Even though the sausage was damaged, the man at the store gave me the refund without a question. He knew my father.

From my father, I learned that personal intensity and a sense of purpose can be communicated through your body posture, your facial expression, and your tone of voice. There emanated from him a sense of brooking no interference with his plans—"taking no shit." Even as I feared and despised his violence, I admired his qualities of improvisation and wholehearted, passionate embracing of the great things of life—the ocean, the outdoors, the uncontrolled wildness in the heart of human beings. I loved the way he handled money. "What the hell?" was his attitude: "I've earned it, I've got it—I spend and enjoy it." As a kid, this attitude meant I loved going out with him. As an adult, I've learned to temper this with my mother's ability to save.

When I was seven or eight, he taught me to do the conga. I had to dance for his friends when they came to visit. Later, standing on his shoes, I learned to waltz, fox trot, and do fancy ballroom dancing. At fifteen, I went with the family to grown-up dances at the Renaissance Ballroom on 138th Street and Seventh Avenue. Dad and Mom were great dancers, and I learned to lindy hop watching them. In exchange, I taught Dad to cha-cha, merengue, and mambo. Then he would whirl me around the floor, showing off all the steps we knew. We danced smoothly without speech; just the pressure of his fingertips told me when to spin out. I smile to think of it. I became an indefatigable dancer; at seventeen, I could dance partners down at Rockland Palace at 155th Street and Eighth Avenue.

Someone said, "To dance is to be in touch with the rhythm of the universe." I believe that. I still love to dance, and I bless my father for it.

And I bless him for his reaction when, at the end of the third grade, a teacher asked me to run for student council secretary. I didn't know what the student council was, so I asked my father, Should I? He said, "What's the question? *Run.*" I ran and won, and that was the beginning of my leadership training. I went on to become vice president of the student council by sixth grade, Leader in seventh and eighth grades, Head of Heads (chief officer in the School Patrol) in ninth grade, member of the student council in high school, president of the senior class, and "Girl Most Likely to Succeed" in twelfth grade. My dad (and mom) never doubted I could do whatever I wanted—so I did.

Dad's deep pride in my accomplishments and those of my sister could be embarrassing. In public places like the subway, he would boom out so that everybody in the car would hear, "So how are you doing in German at Hunter College?" I'd try to whisper a reply, and he'd go on to boom out something about Shakespeare or tennis or zoology. I simply could not fail because of all the public pronouncements Dad made on trains and at family gatherings; I could not do anything but graduate and make him proud.

But Dad's violence against my mother sickened me. It was the chasm that grew between us as I approached adulthood, as he continued to come back to intimidate and hurt my mother for ten years after they separated, driven apart by his temper and his infidelities.

When I was a senior in high school, I confronted Dad after he had hit my mother several times. Overriding my fear and respect for him, I told him, "You are a brute, and I am not afraid of you anymore. You can kill me if you want." He went out of his mind. I, his firstborn, who had never spoken back, made a comment, or shown any disapproval about his violence against my mom or his total disrespect for her with his various women, had called him a brute. He flew into a fury. I lost count of how many times he slapped me. He only stopped when my mom threatened him with a pair of scissors—a first for her, too. He left, and I went to school the next day with a swollen face.

That day, I had to write a qualifying exam for the English prize at graduation. I was tied for the prize with another student, Peter Kacalanos. I wrote incomprehensible babble and, of course, lost to Peter. Miss Mahoney, my English teacher, asked me what was wrong. "Nothing," I said.

But Dad stayed in our lives. One day he reappeared after three weeks' absence, very dark from the sun. I asked, "Where have you been, Daddy?"

He said, "I got in the car and drove to Arizona. The West is something else, baby. You gotta go one day." My mother just stared at him like he was crazy, but I thought, "Wow! What an adventure!"

I had heard of only one other person who had done something like that—a kind of wild woman, a single parent with two boys, who would drive them from Brooklyn to Philadelphia just to buy hamburgers or Philly steaks. I thought, "I *like* that kind of wildness."

Now, I find, what I remember most about Dad is his message of "Go for it, take chances!" I admired his risk taking. He made something of himself, I now see, through sheer courage. Without a high school diploma, he got himself promoted to desk clerk in the refinery where he'd been a laborer. Finding this job too sedentary and missing the camaraderie with "the boys," he went back to the refinery floor and worked as a supervisor for more than twenty years, bossing recent immigrants from Eastern Europe, many of whom had never seen a black man, let alone been supervised by one. He ran his own contracting business on the side, too. As an adult, I realized what strength and forbearance it must have taken for him to keep his temper and his job all those years. His frustration and impatience were misdirected at the women in his life.

What do I make of such a man, such a father, so wonderful in so many ways, so demonic and self-centered in others? I amalgamate in me the best from him—the daring, the joy, and the energy—but control the demonic in me because I've seen how it damages family and self.

The Gift of Endurance

How did Mama endure? For she did endure, without complaints or recriminations, with no word ever spoken to us children against our father. I guess she must have really loved him. They had been children together; their families knew each other. They lived in the Negro apartment house on Twenty-seventh Street (the only building in Hell's Kitchen where black people lived), went to the Hudson Guild community center together, and went to Camp Phoenicia, the summer camp run by the Hudson Guild, although only Mama spoke of the good times at camp with her brothers.

Ruth Cromer Williams, my mother, was short and stout with slightly bowed legs, but she had a special round-faced beauty, with lovely smooth skin, soft, deep-set eyes, and a sharp nose with flared nostrils. She had a mysterious widow's peak, half an inch of hair extending down from her hairline, which she never tried to disguise or remove. She was soft-spoken and not easily moved to anger; she hardly ever spanked me.

Academically, Mama's career growth had been stunted by a high school counselor who let her go with her friends to Central Needle Trades High School instead of a good school like Washington Irving or Julia Richman, where, with her brains, she belonged. Mama was just sixteen when I was born, and for a while she was the only breadwinner in a house of four adults and two kids. She worked for years in a sweatshop behind the Lord & Taylor department store, first making shoulder pads for women's suits and dresses, then crinolines when shoulder pads went out of style. Later she worked at Woolworth's as a counter "girl" and cashier.

She also did piecework in a costume jewelry factory. She worked in the factory five and a half days a week, and I recall smelling the glue each Saturday evening when she did work that she'd brought home on that afternoon to make extra money.

Mama had a budget system, using envelopes marked Rent, Insurance, Gas and Electric, Miscellaneous, and Mr. Kaplan. Every payday she put some money in each envelope so that when the bills came due, she could pay them. Mr. Kaplan was an itinerant salesman who sold curtains, bedspreads, and slipcovers on credit, and we seemed to owe him forever. I know that because through three home addresses—apartments on 118th Street, 121st Street, and Amsterdam Avenue—I answered the bell on Saturdays when he came to collect two dollars or whatever Mama had contracted to pay him weekly.

Once Mr. Kaplan came and Mama was short. Mama knew it was him when the bell rang, and she said, "Tell him I'm not at home."

"Okay, Mama," I said, and dutifully yelled down five floors through the stairwell, "Mr. Kaplan, Mama told me to tell you she's not at home!"

I'm sure he went away laughing. Mama was a long-term customer who always paid whatever she owed, so he wasn't worried.

I don't know where Mama learned to manage money so well. I never quite got her knack for it. If I had, I'm sure I'd be a rich woman now.

Mama's demeanor hid how strong and smart she was. While my father was around, she played second fiddle to him. Dad shone in conversation, exuberance, sense of adventure, social graces, and spending, while Mama was there for him, with his clothes pressed, his favorite meals cooked, the house cleaned, asking no questions about his comings and goings. I guess at first it was worthwhile, because he was there, attentive and loving, but as Dad got into his early thirties, he grew away from Mama and became increasingly abusive.

The abuse was not only physical but psychological. Dad didn't want Mama to have friends over or to visit them. He harangued her with jealous questions whenever she tried to be independent. Once, she signed up for a class in patternmaking and clothing design at George Washington High School, but Dad made her life so miserable with questions— "Where is this class? Who's in it? Why do you need it, anyway? Why were you three minutes late coming home? Are you really going to school?"—that she gave up going; it wasn't worth the inquisition. I'm sure that Dad's cruelty, and Mama's years of not acknowledging the pain she suffered, contributed to the case of colitis that nearly killed her when she was forty-four.

Both Dad and Mama had an entrepreneurial streak. Dad had his contracting business, and Mama bought a stationery and candy store with a woman friend of hers. They were both quite successful businesspeople at first, but both businesses failed in the end. Mama's partner was dipping into the receipts, and Dad was philandering so much that he couldn't attend to business. Mama sold her half of the candy store at break-even or a slight loss and went back to piecework in that shoulder pad factory on West 38th Street, uncomplaining.

Mama and Daddy split up when Mama could no longer take Dad's violence or his constant nagging, arguing, and haranguing. She told him he had to leave. I overheard the argument when Mama asked him to leave the night before my graduation from junior high school. I was shocked that he acceded to her demand. When I woke up for graduation he was gone, around the corner to the apartment where his mistress and her best girlfriend lived. (I hated both women; they were stout and hairy and rough-mannered. What a contrast to Mama!)

Once Dad left, I began almost immediately to see Mama change. She revealed her ability to do things and make smart decisions. Our lives ran very smoothly without the daily apprehension that accompanied my father's surprise visits and his accusations and questions.

I felt sick at heart that I had underestimated and discounted Mama's role in my life, so full of adoration was I for my handsome, charismatic father. And I vowed, "I will not allow any man to hit me. I am not going to go to college to be some man's punching bag." From there, it was a small step to my next resolution never to marry, for I saw around me few happy marriages to change my opinion.

Mama, my sister Ruthie, and I became closer. We enjoyed our Friday-night rituals: fish and spaghetti for dinner and a store-bought dessert treat, first from Cushman's and later from a pastry shop on Amsterdam Avenue between 160th and 161st Streets. Sometimes we went to the movies afterward, but most often we'd play a card game (Coon Can) or watch TV.

Periodically, we'd get a surprise visit from Dad—usually a violent one—or else he'd call and talk *at* Mama for hours on the phone. What could she do about it? An order of protection would only have angered him beyond anything we'd ever witnessed, so Mama took the slaps. Thank God he never punched or kicked her or hit her with things, but his hands were big and tough and swift; I know, because I saw colors whenever his quick hands found my face.

Mama took all of the abuse and went on to get her GED (high school equivalency diploma), so that she could escape working in sweatshops and the five-and-ten. Ruthie tutored her in math and I tutored her in English, and she passed the exam the first time. Ruthie and I were the first to know, because we held the envelope up to the light and read the letter. "Let's make a cake," my sister suggested, and she did, being the good baker that she is, and we rolled up a small piece of paper and tied a ribbon on it to be a diploma.

When Mama came home, we buried the GED letter among the other mail. "Here's the mail, Mama."

"I'll look later," she said. "I'm beat. You girls got supper ready?"

"Yeah, Mama, but maybe you should look at the mail *now*."

"Why are you girls acting so strange?"

"No reason, Mama, but why don't you look?"

"Okay, okay," she said, flopping on the couch. We watched from the kitchen, acting busy at getting supper on the table.

"Girls, girls! Come here—I passed, I passed!" She jumped up off the couch and twirled around and around. "I passed, I passed! Thank God! Thank you, girls!"

"We *thought* you had, Mama, so Ruthie baked a graduation cake and I made the diploma. You're a high school graduate now, Mama!"

"Yes," she said, "and I'm only thirty-eight years old. Now I can take the civil service exams. I'm gonna call Buddy" (Mama's oldest brother, already a successful taker of civil service exams), "and ask his advice."

"But supper first, and then dessert, Mama." We beamed with pride: *Our Mama's a high school graduate!*

Bright as she was, Mama bought review books, studied them, and passed a series of exams that got her a city job in the Department of Social Services. As she rose, she saved her money religiously. She taught me to save, too, and to always have a bank account in my name alone—Dad and one of his mistresses had cleaned out my parents' joint account. Later, after I had been teaching three years, we were able to pool our money and buy a house near Mama's two brothers, Uncle Buddy and Uncle Charlie, in Corona, Queens, New York. It was a two-family house; we had the first floor, the basement, and the yard, and we rented out the apartment upstairs. Mama was beyond happy. She and my sister had house pride; I had yard pride. I remember walking home from the number 7 subway train, turning the corner at 110th Street and Thirty-seventh Avenue, and smelling the horse manure I had put out to make the roses and hydrangeas grow.

Mama's house was her all-in-all. She would have been content forever to clean it, and raise tomatoes, green peppers, string beans, and cukes in the backyard, making frequent visits to her nearby brothers. But her contented, quiet life was interrupted when she nearly died from an ulcerated colon. When she recovered through change of diet and electrolyte corrections, Mama got a new lease on life and a new sense of adventure. She went on trips to Europe with Ruthie, to Hawaii, on lots of cruises, and on bus trips all over the Northeast. She went on this way—enjoying her brothers, sisters, friends, and church—until she was stricken with Alzheimer's.

Mama is now in a home looking blissful, unable to remember the recent past. When I once dared to ask her how she felt when she thought about Dad and his violence, she looked at me and said, "Lorraine, what's the point in even talking about that? It's past. Leave it there." She continued, "You need to go downstairs and see how Charlie and Buddy are doing checking those coats." (Her words meant nothing, however; her brothers, Uncle Charlie and Uncle Buddy, were at home in Queens.)

"Okay, Mama," I replied. "I'll go downstairs and check when I leave." I was thinking, I wish I could skip over the past so easily and so rightly, but the price she is paying for forgetting is one I'm not willing to pay.

My mom's life taught me about planning and moving forward patiently, about winning through simply putting one foot in front of the other. She taught me about the power of prayer, and the power of knowing that God is with me.

And she taught me something simple but vital: the order of the week. Monday to Friday we work, Saturday we do chores and go to the movies, and Sunday we reserve for a special quiet—church, family games, newspaper reading, and a special, early five o'clock dinner. I learned the steadying power of rhythm, ritual, and predictability in life from Mom, and how these simple, holy things are necessary for sanity in both my personal and professional life.

Perhaps these routines saved her. I know they saved me. And now I use the same principle to provide stability and predictability to the lives of the children in the schools where I've worked—qualities many of their lives usually lack.

The Gift of Faith

My mother's mother was a remarkable woman. The women at Father Divine's church called her Sister Nine Babies or Sister Hattie, but we called her Sissy. The future Hattie Bell Cromer was born in a little town in South Carolina, either Liberty or Prosperity. My mother's father, William Cromer, was from one of those towns, too. Sissy left school in the third grade to chop cotton. She and my grandfather Willie met at a dance, courted and married, and had a son, William, known as Buddy.

My grandfather came north after my uncle Buddy was born to find work and a place to live. Once established, he sent for my grandmother and Uncle Buddy, and they came up north on a boat. They lived near the bottom of Manhattan and then moved to 44 West 27th Street. In time, Sissy became pregnant twelve more times, giving birth ten times and finally raising to adulthood eight children, four boys and four girls, all still alive today. After the birth of the tenth child and the refusal of my grandfather to use birth control of any kind, they separated, leaving my grandmother to raise the children alone working as a domestic and taking in laundry.

When I came to know Grandma Sissy, she had moved to Harlem. She lived in a series of apartments—East 116th Street, East 118th Street, and West 115th Street. On East 116th Street, she lived on the top floor of a tenement whose hallways were always dark and smelled dank, like wet cement. Her apartment was always scrupulously clean, despite the fact that seven people shared four rooms—three of her children lived with her, plus a huge woman and her two sons.

When my sister and I spent an occasional weekend at Sissy's we thought it fun to be among lots of kids, all crowded together. Sometimes we slept three or four girls to a bed, lying head to toe, talking and giggling until a grown-up threatened, "You kids shut up and go to sleep before I come in there." Of course, we then whispered under the covers. In the mornings, we ate breakfast at a sideboard in the dining room, which doubled as a bedroom. Usually we had coffee and milk (illicit and unheard-of at home, making it one of the great treats of the visit) and a sausage sandwich.

Dinner was a wonderful affair, ending always with homemade dessert: a "one, two, three" pound cake that Sissy "just stirred up" in a big bowl in her lap, or, in the summer, homemade ice cream made in a wooden hand-turned churn. We ate at a huge oak dining room table that could expand to fit whatever number came. I thought the table was magic. It took me a few years to figure out that the table had leaves. The table got away from the family somehow and was replaced by a spindly-legged modern table with no magic.

Sissy belonged to Father Divine's church, a remarkable Harlem institution in those days. Father Divine was a charismatic black man who attracted mostly blue-collar women to his congregation—factory workers and domestics, most of whom had children and other relations they were supporting and caring for single-handedly. Whatever his teachings, Father Divine created a church that provided the sense of community all good organizations provide. It was a place where hardworking, embattled women felt special and needed. Each had a role to play and work to do at church on Sundays; they wore special uniforms (green suits, white blouses, green tams, and white shoes) and they were fed delicious, inexpensive meals. I remember, as a child, enjoying the food, the music, and above all the pageantry of the charismatic services, during which spirit-filled women and men would faint, dance, and speak in tongues.

To this community of believers, Sissy brought her strong belief that God is a force working in your life for good and that He will take care of you if you trust in Him and do right. Sissy and I often talked about God and the ways He worked in our lives. She told me that I was blessed, and I believed her.

Sissy worked hard, though she received scanty wages and less respect from the people she worked for. She knew the intimate details of the lives of the white people she served, but they knew little and cared to know little about her. Once when I was eleven or twelve I went with her to the home of a family she worked for near Riverside Drive on the West Side of Manhattan. While I walked toward the main entrance, she veered off toward a side gate. I asked, "Sissy, where are you going? Here's the front door."

She answered, "I can't go in that way. I go in through this gate here."

I read the sign and it said, "Delivery Entrance." As she disappeared through the gate, I promised myself that I would *never* go through a delivery gate. Only much later did I realize that her inner sense of self was somehow unshaken by the system that forced her for almost two decades to go through the delivery entrance. The insanity of racism leaves me wordless even now. I have seen too much of the world and people to believe in the inherent, unearned superiority of any person or race. But to prevail with faith and sense of self intact is Sissy's legacy to me.

She died—needlessly, I think—at age eighty-nine. For years she had been on kidney dialysis, and she had high blood pressure. Just before Christmas, she was diagnosed as having a "blocked bowel." A relative gave permission for an operation, and Sissy died from complications.

Just before her death, as I was driving to work one morning, a voice said to me, "Drive to the hospital and see Sissy *now!*"

"Now?" I questioned the voice.

"Now!" came the reply, so I turned the car around, parked illegally somewhere on the crowded streets near the hospital, and managed to get in to visit Sissy outside of the usual visiting hours by saying I had driven from out of state.

I found Sissy lying in bed with her eyes closed, tubes running out of everywhere tubes can run. I took her hand and spoke in her ear, "I am here, Sissy. It's Lorraine. I love you, and I thank you for all you taught me and for your many blessings. Do you hear me?"

Ever so gently, she squeezed my hand. Then I said to her what she used to say to me: "Peace and many blessings."

On my way out of the hospital, I met the doctor, a young intern, who had operated on Sissy. I said to him, "My grandmother had a blocked bowel. Was there no alternative to an operation?" He looked blankly at me, without answering.

More forcefully, I asked, "If this had been *your* mother or grand-mother, would you have operated?" He began to stutter words that made no sense. I left him explaining something to the air.

Sissy died during the night. I ask for her guidance and blessings still.

The Gift of Quiet

F inally, I must tell you about my father's father, Edward Lewis Williams—Grandpa Ed to me. He owned a little farm in Potters' Crossing, New Jersey. Watching him catch a chicken for dinner, swing it in the air, and finally snap its head off was a regular Sunday spectacular for me during the summers I spent on his farm. I wasn't so much horri-fied at the sight of the chicken bouncing around the yard without a head as I was awed by Grandpa's tremendous strength and dispassionate manner while doing this. The way Miss Ida, my step-grandmother, would chop the chickens' heads off with a hatchet on a block paled in comparison to Grandpa's *swing, swing, swing, snap.*

Grandpa was a huge man. He stood about 6'3" weighed over 250 pounds, and had huge hands and big, broad feet (he wore size 13½ EEE shoes). Yet he was a gentle giant, a man whose life was governed by hard work and high moral values. Throughout the community, people called him Big Wheel because of his power and influence: he got out the vote for the Democratic Party in Potters' Crossing while quietly amassing wealth by making Celotex wallboard, running his own fish and produce business, and buying and selling small pieces of property.

In addition, he served as a deacon in the local Foot Wash Baptist Church. Watching Grandpa humble himself to wash another deacon's feet in church, reenacting one of Christ's last acts on earth, moved him to another place in my heart.

Grandpa loved to be quiet. He was an assiduous newspaper reader, and listening to the news on the radio, especially his favorite commentator, Gabriel Heatter, was a nightly ritual.

Years after our summer farm days, Gramps was forced to sell his house, supposedly because of urban renewal. However, nothing has been built on Gramps' old property, and I believe his resistance to indoor plumbing—he preferred his old two-seater outhouse back by the pond at the edge of the property—may have prompted neighbors to complain. So he and his wife were relocated to a two-story government-built house with indoor plumbing, neighbors visible on all sides, no trees, no porch, and only a postage-stamp-sized backyard.

In this spirit-killing environment, Grandpa endured a series of strokes, each more weakening than the one before, until it was impossible for him to go on existing—I won't say *living*—in that barren little house. He was placed in a home, "one of the best," they said, thanks to Grandpa's Democratic Party connections. He lasted nearly a year there.

Once when I visited him he said, "Hello, baby! It's worth a million dollars in pennies to see you." He was strapped in a chair—my powerful Gramps was diapered and strapped to a chair. The last time I saw him alive, he was in intensive care in a twilit room where the only sound was the hum of life-preserving machines. As I stood at his bedside, I placed my heart somewhere beyond feeling; I knew my Grandpa wasn't there.

A week later, when I got the call that Gramps had died, I threw myself on my bed and stayed there for twenty-four hours. Only through writing poems about him was I able to close, partially, the hole left by his passing.

THE FUNERAL

His purple-grey face lay cushioned in serge, satin, and dark mahogany,
The flowers' sweet intermixed with repressed scent of decay.
He and I heard the hymn sung out of tune,
Heard lies made of the truths of his life,
Emptied of flesh and meaning,
Heard a eulogy by a friend who defined him in five minutes.
I smiled: eighty-six years defined in five minutes.
After the long sermon
(The Lord be with you)
By a man who scarcely knew him
(And with your spirit)
I saw hot tears flash
(The Lord giveth)
In eyes that never loved him
(And the Lord taketh away).
Then I could have sworn he uneased a little, and sighed
(Blessed be the name of the Lord).
I knew that he understood and forgave.
And I offered him then my final tribute: dry eyes.

As children, when Ruthie and I were not with Gramps in the summer, he would write me long letters, telling me about what he was thinking as he listened to the rain on the farmhouse roof and watched the wind in the trees. As an adolescent, I found his musings corny and never thought to save the letters. But life has a strange way of salvaging what you have wasted or thought worthless. Today, I realize that part of Grandpa's legacy to me has been the love of quiet and sitting on a porch listening to the rain, sensing the ocean-like smell of the earth and the motion of the tops of trees as the wind walks over them.

In my life and work, I call on my grandfather as an ancestor to guide me with his lessons of patience, wisdom, and quiet.

∾

Today, I am boundlessly grateful to all of my family for being who they were, in all of their humanness. I was deeply loved by both of my parents, even when they stopped loving each other. And the faith that both Sissy and Grandpa Ed expressed in me assured me that I was treasured.

The strength I got from these four remarkable people enables me to move ahead in life, no matter what obstacles and troubles I may face.

On Attitude

Life ain't fair—but it can be beautiful!

~

Work hard—deserve to play hard.

~

Daily reflection on your efforts and outcomes will improve both.

~

Avoid people who envy, complain, and drain.

~

When you work in a place where your efforts are belittled, save yourself—leave! But until you leave, continue to do impeccable work. Otherwise, you become like your detractors.

CHAPTER 3

Glimpses of the World

FIRST LESSONS IN LIVING,

LEARNING, AND LEADING

In the first half of the first grade, I learned to read Dick and Jane, that universal American text relevant to no one. I don't remember how I learned to read, but I did, and that's all I remember from P.S. 10 at 117th Street and St. Nicholas Avenue. Because my family moved, I was transferred to P.S. 157 on 126th Street for the second half of the first grade, and there I met Miss Katz. She lives in my memory, first, because she let me read whatever I wanted while she taught the others Dick and Jane. (My favorites were the Disney books about Donald Duck and his nephews, Huey, Dewey, and Louie.) More important, Miss Katz lives in my memory because of my lunch tragedy and the way she handled it.

My mom one day had fixed my most favorite lunch ever, the one I still crave at crucial times: bologna on white bread with mustard, a Red Delicious apple, and a package of Yankee Doodles. (If you haven't had the pleasure of eating a Yankee Doodle, you should know that it's a chocolate cupcake with a dollop of "cream" in the middle. It is eaten by breaking it open like an egg and smearing the cream over all the cake so that each bite can be savored with the requisite amount of cream. When I was a kid, if I was a little frantic, I would also chew the paper cup the Yankee Doodle came in.)

Anyway, I stowed this wonderful lunch in the sliding-door clothing closet near my seat in row six of Miss Katz's classroom. The smell of bologna and mustard buoyed me all morning. When noon came around, Miss Katz in her usual routine called each row in turn: "Row 1, Row 2 . . . Row 6, go to the closet to get your clothing and your lunch." When I heard "Row 6," I bolted to the closet and went to where I had put my lunch. NO LUNCH. I frantically ran up and down the whole closet looking—still no lunch. I threw myself into my seat, put my head on the desk, and sobbed.

Naturally, Miss Katz came over asking, "What's wrong, Lorraine?"

I blubbered, "Lunch—my lunch—somebody stole my lunch!"

Miss Katz said, "Stop crying. I'll take care of it." I wiped my tears away as she put me at the front of the line. When the rest of the class was dismissed, she took me to get the teachers' lunch. This was so special that I remember thinking, "Maybe I'll lose my lunch tomorrow."

Being Tolerated

In the third grade, I met Miss Janet White, a very pale, elegant teacher with a pleasant, soft kind of lantern jaw and a cleft chin. I vividly remember following her around for two months while she had lunchtime yard duty. I ate lunch fast so I could be with her. We held memorable conversations: "What are we going to do this afternoon, Miss White? That was a good story you read us this morning. You going to read again this afternoon? We going to the nature room tomorrow, Miss White? What did I get on the arithmetic test?" She patiently answered all my questions for two months until for some reason I detached myself one day and went out to run and play donkey (a ball game), double dutch, and other rope and ball games with the other kids.

Why I needed to be with Miss White, I did not and do not know. And why she did not chase me away to play with the normal kids but instead tolerated me and filled my unspoken need, I also don't know. I do know that both Miss Katz's allowing me to read what I wanted and Miss White's allowing me to be in her presence have been part of my own teaching practice since I was a twenty-one-year-old novice.

I've already mentioned my next memorable teacher—Mr. James Cooper, a sartorially splendid African-American man. He was tall and wore steel-rimmed glasses, a gray pinstriped double-breasted suit, and wing-tipped shoes. He was sharp, smart, and well-spoken, and from fourth to sixth grade I had a crush on him. He was the one who singled me out and said, "You should run for student council secretary." I did and won. What an amazing privilege it was for me. I learned to take notes, write minutes, read them to the council, accept amendments, and incorporate them. By the sixth grade, I had developed leadership skills that have carried me to the present.

Also in the third grade, I met the school librarian, Miss Brez. The library was on the top floor. It had a huge skylight, and Miss Brez had placed a wicker chintz-covered couch and two wicker chairs beneath the skylight. I fell in love with reading on the couch with the sunlight pouring down on me and the pages of the book like a blessing. To this day, I love reading in the sun.

Miss Brez let me take books home over the weekend against school policy, "provided you keep them clean." So when we studied China, I did extra reading about Chinese life and Chinese writing, which fascinated me as art. I spent hours at home, dreamily copying Chinese characters for the look and sweep of them.

An Opening World

think it was Miss White who took the class to New York's great American Museum of Natural History to extend our third-grade study of the

Plains Indians. I remember being impressed with the size of the vast lobby with its vaulted ceiling, the big Indian war canoe, the Northwest Indians' totems, the stuffed moose with their horns locked in eternal combat, and the Alaskan brown bear with a freshly caught salmon at his feet.

We wound up in the planetarium. It was cold, maybe to suggest the chill of interstellar space. Then they turned the lights out for the star show, and some boys and girls were kissing, but no boy kissed me. I decided that the planetarium was an awful place. I was cold and unkissed. I never returned to the planetarium.

But then we went to the auditorium to see nature films. I am sure that the teacher had to kill time, the Plains Indians and planetarium having gone by too quickly. This time when the lights went out, I knew I wouldn't be kissed, but I didn't care because I loved movies. The films were about animals, their habits and habitats. One film showed a foal being born. I cried silently at the care and attention the mother horse gave to the spindly-legged foal, cleaning it and nudging it to stand and hovering near so that it could find the teat to suck. Well, now, I thought, *here* was the reason for the trip.

Later, Miss White let me in on a secret. "You know," she said, "they show films at the museum every Saturday afternoon, and you don't need a teacher or grown-up to come here." So most Saturdays for years my sister and I went to the American Museum of Natural History to see films.

The Spirit Killers

The first bump in elementary school came in the fourth grade, when I had Miss Fenster. She was short and stoutish, had bulbous eyes and thin, mousy unkempt hair, and never taught us anything. She, up to that time, was my least favorite teacher.

One lazy afternoon, when Miss Fenster was extra-specially unprepared, she said, "Put everything away—clear your desks. Now, I have a question. Why are colored people's palms white, not colored?" The class fell silent. I looked at my hands and noticed for the first time that indeed my palms were not the same color as the tops of my hands. I discovered this with wonder and some sense of embarrassment and even stupidity, because I had no explanation or answer to give her. I sat looking down at my hands as the other kids offered explanations that apparently they had heard somewhere. I can't remember what they were, but I remember that they all involved derogatory and stereotypic beliefs about African-Americans being slow and late. I felt bad but somehow very glad that for the first time in four years of schooling, I could not join in the class discussion.

She was the first teacher I ever hated.

But in the sixth grade, I had Mrs. Johnson. Ugh! How I hated and feared her. She taught me one thing: that fear and hate work for control, but not for love of learning. Under Mrs. Johnson, for the first time, I learned to produce out of fear.

She was a tall, big-boned, broad-hipped African-American woman, with bulbous eyes that gleamed with malevolent joy, especially when she was punishing one of us.

In Mrs. Johnson's class, humiliation was a frequent event, but there were three humiliations that I especially recall. The first one happened to me.

In previous grades, I had learned to multiply, and I'd been taught to write the number to be carried, small, near the number it was to be added to. Mrs. Johnson didn't like this. She explained to the class that since this was the sixth grade, we should hold the number to be carried in our heads. I heard her, but a habit dies hard, and my fear of Mrs. Johnson made matters worse. When she sent me to the board, I was so determined to get the right answer, I forgot to carry the numbers in my head. Instead, I wrote them.

When Mrs. Johnson looked at my work, she gasped. Everybody looked down. "Lorraine," she declared, "you defied me. You deliberately wrote those numbers when I told you not to. Come here, young lady."

Like a person going to her execution, I approached her desk. "Hold out your right hand"—she took out her 18-inch ruler—"and don't flinch," and she hit my palm three times. No one had ever struck me except my parents. It hurt, but I didn't, wouldn't cry, wouldn't give her the satisfaction, wouldn't lose face in front of the kids that I'd known since first grade. I could feel they were rooting for me to take the pain and the shame and not break. She'd struck others before who'd flinched and cried, but I didn't.

"Take your seat," she said, sounding disappointed. What she didn't and couldn't know was that from that day forward I hated her, and I knew that somewhere, somehow, someday I would get her back.

The second humiliation was far worse than mine. Alex Wright had a bladder problem. He'd brought a note from his mom asking teachers to let him go to the bathroom whenever he requested. We all knew his problem, but we respected him because he was smart and a nice kid, too. One day in the middle of some math busywork, Alex raised his hand to be excused. He kept his hand raised for one, two, three, four minutes. Mrs. Johnson made no acknowledgment. The fifth minute, Alex got out of his seat and stood by her desk. She still did not acknowledge him. Finally, he peed a large puddle at the foot of her desk.

Now Mrs. Johnson acknowledged him. She pushed her desk away from the expanding pool of pee and yelled, "You filthy boy—how dare you! Now, go get a mop and mop it up!" Deep collective hate for her rolled through the room. If we had been bad, unafraid kids, we would have run crazy. Each of us felt for Alex.

The third humiliation I remember was the last straw. Ralph Jefferson's mom had died during the summer leaving him, his younger brother, and his father forlorn. The father was in such deep grief and, I guess, had so few skills as a parent that Ralph came to school unwashed, wearing filthy shirts. Mrs. Johnson was pitiless. Each day, she made loud comments about how dirty and ill-kept Ralph was. While we all looked down, feeling pity for Ralph's loss and her cruel remarks, he never reacted but sat wrapped in dry-eyed sorrow.

Sweet Revenge

Gotta get her, gotta get her," I thought each time she hit a kid or came up behind someone and drilled her long index finger into the space between the collarbone and the shoulder blade. One day at last, a golden opportunity came to get Mrs. Johnson.

One day, she asked me to come up early from lunch to wash the blackboards. It was my custom to eat lunch and then run to the corner candy store to supplement the nutritious school lunch with grape soda, squirrel nuts, and especially sour pickles, chosen from a jar by size according to your pocket change—three cents, four cents, or five cents, which bought the biggest. I came up to wash the boards, happily filled with grape soda and squirrel nuts and with one hand grasping an extravagant five-cent sour pickle, wrapped in a piece of wax paper, which was getting soggy. I had no thought of doing anything except washing the boards, which I did immediately.

With ten minutes left before the other kids came up, I realized that I had this huge uneaten pickle, and an idea came to me. I thought, "Mrs. Johnson hates pickles and the smell of them." So quickly, with my pencil, I drilled a hole in the end of the pickle and walked around her desk, squeezing the juice all over the floor nearby. When I was finished, I opened the windows to dry the floors, threw the incriminating, squeezed-out pickle down five stories to the street, rinsed my hands in the blackboard water basin, and went downstairs to join my classmates.

Around 12:45, we'd assembled in the classroom, and Mrs. Johnson walked in and went to the board to write our busywork for the afternoon. I was hunched over my work, writing, when I heard her roar, "*I smell pickle*! I smell it, and I will find out who has it. I feel sorry, very sorry for the possessor of that pickle! Take out your things. I'm coming around."

She searched the room three times and turned up no pickle, each time declaring, "I smell it! I know it's in this room and *I will find it*!" Finally, she gave up, grumbling, "Whoever has it: I will find you out before this school day is over." But she never did.

I was so happy, I never thought to wonder whether some innocent passerby on St. Nicholas Avenue had been hit by a well-squeezed pickle.

Shakespeare, Dickens, and Mrs. Ischol

When I graduated from P.S. 157, I looked forward to going to Junior High School 81 although I had never seen it. It's funny the circumscribed life I led. Home and school—a pretty straight run between 121st Street and Manhattan Avenue and 126th Street and St. Nicholas Avenue. From the fifth grade, when we moved to 159th Street, the run was out of the subway at 125th Street, one block to school, and, later, back to 159th Street. There was never any need to go south to 120th Street. So at the summer's end it was a whole new experience when I came out of the subway at 124th Street, walked along St. Nicholas to 120th Street, and turned left to go to the school.

J.H.S. 81 was an imposing, all-girl school—way bigger than my old elementary school. In the seventh grade, I had Miss Masterson for English. She was short and small, wore her gray hair in a bun, and favored classic "school teacher shoes"—Enna Jetticks. In her classroom every inch of available wall space, including the closet doors, was covered with didactic printed material: the eight parts of speech, the four kinds of sentences, prefixes, suffixes, punctuation marks, Greek and Latin roots, and wise sayings ("He who steals my purse steals trash . . . "), all of which we were made to memorize. There were no pictures of any kind to distract us. If we didn't find Miss Masterson interesting, we could always entertain ourselves by perusing the walls. So by the end of the seventh grade I knew the walls very well.

In the eighth grade, Miss Carolyn Dennis introduced me to Shakespeare. We read *Julius Caesar* line by line, just as I did later with Professor Wheeler at Hunter College and as I ultimately taught it when I returned to J.H.S. 81 as a twenty-one-year-old teacher. Miss Dennis made us memorize and recite memorable lines from *Julius Caesar*, and she added subordinating and coordinating conjunctions and independent and dependent clauses to my life.

Mrs. Charlotte Ischol, my ninth-grade English teacher and the school librarian, had varicose veins. At the time, I had no idea what they were, but she remained seated a lot with one leg wrapped in a bandage and resting on an open desk drawer. I learned from Mrs. Ischol to love diagramming sentences. If I did my grammar exercises quickly, I could choose a book to read while the others worked. When all had finished, Mrs. Ischol would say, "Girls, I want to read you a section of a book that just came in," and at the end of the period, the bibliophiles among us would race up to be first to borrow it. She introduced us to Dickens, and at once he became my favorite author. He is still one of my favorites.

Mrs. Ischol made another lasting contribution to my intellectual life. "Lorraine," she said one day, "here are some reduced-price tickets to a repertory theater on East Houston Street. Maybe you and your family could use them."

"Thanks," I said, although I didn't know what a repertory theater was. I don't think I'd ever been to a theater. I went home and talked to my mom about going. Mama bought season tickets for me, my sister, and herself. I think they cost $3.95 for three plays. Even as a fourteen-year-old, I realized what a financial sacrifice this was from Mama's piecework pay.

Our first play was a Sunday matinee. We found East Houston Street, way downtown on what is called the Lower East Side, a neighborhood of lofts, tenements, and old factories that would become artistic and fashionable only many years later. We rode an open freight elevator up to the theater, which must have seated all of seventy-five people. The play was Shakespeare's *Twelfth Night.* We read the playbill, and when the lights slowly dimmed, I heard a rumbling sound as the revolving stage turned and the curtains opened onto the first scene.

I was hooked forever. I've never forgotten the ludicrous crossed yellow garters of Malvolio. Later that season, we saw the old comedy *Arsenic and Old Lace,* and adopted the catchword "Charge!" as a slogan we'd say to provoke laughter and encourage one another in forging ahead over minor obstacles. The whole experience of witnessing theater was life-changing for me. To this day, as an educator, I believe deeply in making the arts a priority in our schools, even when resources are limited.

Tears for Quixote

I studied Spanish under Miss Isabel Fleuranges, a young but old-fashioned, solid, and serious teacher who loved her native language and taught it well and passionately. She took us to see a foreign film—a somewhat exotic experience in those days. "No English is spoken," she told us. "It is *Don Quixote de la Mancha,* a novel written by Cervantes. You'll love it."

Beforehand, the concept puzzled me. I reasoned, "How can I know what's going on? No English is spoken." I relaxed when the movie began and I saw the subtitles.

I was enjoying Don Quixote's misadventures and Sancho Panza's down-to-earth observations, when I was startled to hear someone weeping. I looked to my left and saw Miss Fleuranges crying. I was embarrassed by this sign of what I at that moment deemed weakness, so I looked away and pretended not to have heard or seen her cry. Not until years later, when I saw the musical *Man of La Mancha,* did I realize why she had cried: it was the poignancy of idealism mistaken for madness. I've wept many times about this, too.

Tormenting the Teacher

At some point in either the seventh or eighth grade we were briefly assigned a spanking-brand-new young teacher. Being bright youngsters but not necessarily kind youngsters, we led her a merry chase. She tried to teach us Longfellow's very long poem *Evangeline*. With resignation we daily trooped to English class to be utterly bored in the Acadian forests.

The fun began when she decided to teach us the personal pronouns in the nominative case. We already knew these from Miss Masterson, but she plowed on. "Repeat after me," she said. "I, you, he, she, it, we, you, they." So we repeated them in chorus.

Then, neophyte that she was, she said, "I want each of you to repeat them, and we'll go around the room." There were thirty-six of us, and after the sixth girl had recited, we all caught the rhythm of it:

"I, you, he—

SHEEEIT!—

we! you! they!"

Of course, we were highly amused by the fact that the elided "she, it" sounded like an outrageous, forbidden curse word. As the chant rolled around the room, we accented the *sheeeit*! part louder and more emphatically. The teacher turned beet-red, but she couldn't stop us: we were doing what she'd asked. This was our last lesson in personal pronouns, however.

Cooking and Cleaning

In those days, "smart" girls were not given a course in typing; that was a subject for non-college-bound girls (women to whom I have subsequently paid thousands of dollars to type my papers). All of us were given home economics, however—cooking and housekeeping. Whose wisdom dictated that typing wasn't universally important but cooking and cleaning were?

Anyway, in home economics the class was split in half: one half learned to cook and the other half learned to clean. I shudder now when I think of the colossal waste of intellectual time in these classes. I already knew how to cook; I had to learn because Mama worked, and I had been "starting supper"—buying groceries, peeling and boiling potatoes, and getting vegetables ready—since I was nine years old. I'm sure I wasn't the only student with this kind of experience. Nonetheless, we spent a whole double period (90 minutes) learning to make cocoa. How did those teachers ingeniously expand making cocoa into a 90-minute exercise? This is how: "Copy the recipe into your Home Economics notebook. . . . Get out the required utensils. . . . Measure out the ingredients. . . . Turn on the stove. . . . Put the ingredients into a pot. . . . Cook. . . ." It hurts my head to recall this.

In later classes, we learned to make scrambled eggs and then the last, "advanced" recipe, creamed tuna on toast. This latter I came to love, substituting salmon and fixing it whenever I had a chance to make lunch at home. The repetition finally drove my father to say, "Don't fix no more damned salmon on toast!"

Despite its inanity, we loved to go to cooking. It was cleaning the mock apartment next door to the kitchen that made us all feel like "retards." The apartment was always clean because several classes before us had already cleaned it. Still, we were asked to clean the clean bathroom, dust the dusted furniture, sweep and mop the swept and mopped floors, and finally unmake the made beds and remake them. Apparently, no teacher questioned the insanity of this class. Once one of us girls said out loud, "This is stupid." The rest of us tacitly agreed, but we kept doing it because, to our little eighth-grade minds, "This is better than sitting in some old boring class where you can't talk or move around."

The Magic of Mrs. Graves

We then were assigned to millinery, taught by our homeroom teacher, Mrs. Stella M. Graves, who also was our guidance advisement teacher. She was a stern, take-no-prisoners teacher, built in the solid stereotyped way of teachers—big and rotund at the top and broad-hipped at the bottom. She could make a magic *whish-whish* sound when she walked that I later discovered I could make myself; it was the sound of thighs rubbing against each other in panty hose. We were scared of her, so we learned what she taught us: to stitch little hat-shaped pin cushions and then our very own Easter bonnets. All of this done in silence.

Mrs. Graves invited a dozen of us to her home for tea one Sunday. Mama told me, "You can go, provided you can take your sister." (Ruthie was nine at the time.) Mrs. Graves consented to this, so off we went, traveling deep into Brooklyn on the D train to the subway stop at Kingston and Throop Streets. As Ruthie and I walked to Mrs. Graves's home, at 1511A President Street, we found we had entered a world that was a far cry from our own poor neighborhood. We were impressed by the stately brownstones, the tree-lined streets, the cleanliness and quiet. At 1511A, we walked up a long flight of stairs and entered a home with Oriental rugs, a huge Persian cat, antique chairs (Mrs. Graves cautioned, "Don't sit on those"), a grand piano, a separate dining room, and even an upstairs—like houses in the movies! "Wow," I thought. "My teacher—a black lady—owns this!"

Mrs. Graves invited us to sit around the dining table. She brought a silver tray with the tea fixings, put out delicate, matching china cups and saucers, and brought out a silver platter with finger sandwiches. My sister and I marveled over these, wondering how many made a "real" sandwich; to research this question, I mashed six together. Mrs. Graves caught me doing this but said nothing.

Mrs. Graves put her napkin on her lap, and we twelve quickly followed her lead. She poured tea and passed it around, and we sedately sipped, just as we saw her doing. I sat wondering what all this was really about when Mrs. Graves said, "Girls, I'd like you to go around the table and say what you intend doing when you get out of college."

"Out of college?" I thought. "I'm trying to get out of the eighth grade." But we all went around the table saying things like, "I will go to medical school or law school or teach," while Mrs. Graves nodded approvingly. She was the first teacher to whom we spoke our dreams, and she forced us to make the assumption that we would indeed graduate from college.

She kept us coming out to Brooklyn right through the twelfth grade. We often brought our mothers. We had to design entertaining and didactic programs. We became the AEL Club, named after Anna E. Lawson, our highly respected principal.

After we graduated from high school—as Mrs. Graves had assumed we would—she got her sorority sisters to form their own club, the Xinos. They kept us coming to their brownstones in Brooklyn during our college years, taking us to the theater and on trips and having black women who had "made it" address us. Ultimately, we each graduated from college and became professional women in New York City, thanks largely to Mrs. Graves. Her legacy I continue to this day.

Turning No into Yes

In the ninth grade in J.H.S. 81, getting into one of the specialized public high schools was my biggest objective. I took the test, hoping to get into either the Bronx High School of Science or Hunter College High School, two prestigious schools from which many well-known people had graduated. When the test results arrived, I was distraught—my math score was too low, and it would keep me out of the elite schools.

I had had my heart set on being accepted to at least one of them. Now what could I do? I went to see my counselor. "A small honor school has just opened at the High School of Commerce on West 65th Street," she told me. "It's called the Lincoln Park Honor School. Why not apply there? You've got a good chance of getting in."

"I'll think about it," I told her, but I wasn't cheered up by the prospect.

Fortunately, my English teacher, Mrs. Ischol, saw my sadness. "What's the matter, Lorraine?" she asked as I lingered after class the next day.

"I didn't get into any of the specialized high schools," I said. "I feel so bad."

"Come over here," she said, and we stood by the window and stared out into 120th Street. "What other option do you have?" she asked.

"Well," I said, "I could go to the new honor school at Commerce, but I don't—"

She interrupted me. "Look at it this way, Lorraine: at Science or Hunter, you'd be a little fish in a big pond. In this new school, you could be a big fish in a little pond. Think about it. With your brains and gifts, you'd probably do well there. I'd consider going there if I were you."

I did, and what a difference it made. Although the Lincoln Park Honor School, as I discovered, wasn't nearly as demanding as it could and should have been, those of us who went there were perceived and treated as special. That in itself was important in keeping me focused on school and learning as important elements in my life. In retrospect, I guess the noes from Hunter and Science became the first noes in my life that turned into yeses.

Four Years of Friendships

As it turned out, I breezed through high school. Most of us in the honor school had wanted to go to one of the specialized high schools but had been rejected because of a poor math or English score.

We were housed on the second floor at Commerce High School, separate from the "regular" kids. For the first semester, we shared the basement cafeteria with the other students, which was pure theater. It was a grungy, noisy, poorly lit place where kids fought and where I learned to blow straws at the ceiling and green peas at my friends. Because we were "better" than the other kids, however, we were moved to our own clean, well-lighted cafeteria the second semester.

We never discussed or thought about the superior treatment we received or what the kids left below must have felt. But getting special treatment made us behave specially; in our new cafeteria, we ceased blowing straws and peas and sat and talked quietly, as befitted the well-lighted, clean environment.

I loved being fifteen and slim and laughing at all the wonderfulness of high school. Having been with girls only for the previous three years hadn't prepared me for fifteen-year-old boys, who were shy and raucous and lewd: "Hey, Lorraine," said Richie, "there are two good points about that sweater."

Naively, I replied, "Really, what are they?"

"Haw, haw, ha, ha," was the answer. Finally I got it and blushed. So silly, those boys, yet fascinating. Richie was the first boy in high school to ask me out dancing at the Palladium. I had to say no—I wasn't allowed to date solo—but the group dates make up some of my best memories of high school.

Every holiday and every Regents exam break my friends and I hung out together. We went bowling—one boy worked in an alley and his boss let him set pins for us for free if we rented the shoes.

We went to shows at Radio City Music Hall. We could be the first ones in for the special Christmas and Easter shows if our friend Amy got there real early to buy us tickets. She almost always did; Amy was happy for any excuse to escape her home and her father, who so hated Amy's multiracial friends that he would go down into his apartment building's basement when we used to visit and stay there until we left.

We rode the Jersey Central ferry across the Hudson River between Chambers Street in lower Manhattan and Jersey City, riding back and forth and back and forth but paying only one fare, because we never got off.

We sat in Horn & Hardart, the famous old Automat restaurant with dishes behind little glass doors, pooled our change, and bought beans, macaroni and cheese, sandwiches, and pastry.

Life with my high school friends was full of laughter and jokes about each other, other kids, and our teachers. We rarely spoke of the reality of our home lives. We raced to school early every morning to meet by a balcony radiator in the auditorium to rehash the previous night's TV programs. "How about when Sid Caesar and Imogene Coca did this?" "Or when Lucy did that?" "Or when Ralph Kramden said this?" And we'd laugh as hard as we had when we'd seen them the night before; the sharing was so delicious.

I did enough schoolwork to graduate, but I wasn't challenged. I remember liking biology, loving choir, enjoying Spanish. I loved to read, so English was a snap. So little was required of me that I had plenty of time to read books that interested me. I read lots about Africa because I wanted to be a medical missionary like Albert Schweitzer. I also read nearly every book listed on the back of the Great Illustrated Classics published by Dodd, Mead.

I did fail one course—Regents trigonometry—and came close to failing in chemistry, too. Near the end of the year, Mr. Abrahams, my chemistry teacher, told me, "Miss Williams, you haven't a clue about this subject. You can't balance equations. You break test tubes over the Bunsen burner. You fail tests. You're going to flunk this course."

"I can't," I protested. "I need it to graduate."

"Okay," he said. "Let's make a deal. I'll give you whatever grade you get on the state Regents exam."

"Deal," I said. I took out my Regents review book and I went through it three times, taking the old exams and memorizing the answers from the back of the book. I got an 85 on the Regents—a minor miracle. I really didn't know any chemistry; I knew answers to questions. The wonder and awe of science were lost on me.

One day during my senior year, my counselor called me down to her office. "You don't want to come to school for a test this Saturday, do you?" she asked.

"Nah," I said. "A test on Saturday? No, thank you."

"Okay," she said.

When I came to school that Monday, my friend Amy said to me, "Where were you Saturday? Why didn't you come for the test?"

"The test? What test?" I asked, pretending ignorance since she seemed so surprised that I wasn't there.

"The Regents Scholarship exam," Amy replied. I felt stupid. Why hadn't I gone? Why hadn't the counselor told me the importance of the test? I never quite forgave her.

Later, the same counselor informed me that I could graduate somewhat early. "You have enough credits to graduate six months early," she said.

I went home and asked my mom what I should do. "How do you feel about it, Lorraine?"

I looked at Mama. Knowing how hard she was working to support us girls and all the abuse she was taking from our father, I decided I had to get launched into real life as soon as I could. So as much as I wanted to go on being with my high school friends, I went back and told the counselor yes.

When I graduated, a semester ahead of my classmates, I wept loudly—not with joy but with sadness, because I was leaving my friends behind.

On Perseverance

Often, the evidence of success is slow in coming or impossible to see. Therefore, much good work must be done by faith and by faith alone.

~

When a near-impossible assignment comes along, take it as a challenge and work like hell to succeed. But instead of results, attach your heart to *significant actions.*

~

Consistency and perseverance beat running from fad to fad.

~

In the face of inept administration or nonsensical bureaucracy, people desperately need confirmation that they are not crazy to go on believing, demanding, caring.

~

If you're successful, you'll be envied and you'll make enemies. But go on! Because the alternative is death.

~

Keep asking, "Why not?" till you run out of excuses and fear.

CHAPTER 4

"You Can't Outrun Your Fate"

FINDING A PERSONAL MISSION

How proud I was to open our mailbox one day in my upper senior year to find a letter of acceptance to Hunter College.

Hunter was and still is one of the quality four-year colleges that is part of the public City University of New York, at that time a tuition-free system for city residents. I had not applied to any other college, nor had I been advised to. Certainly going away to college outside of New York City never entered my mind, and my counselor never suggested it.

At the time, I never questioned the poor counseling I was receiving. I only knew that in New York City, being able to tell anybody that you were going to Hunter College meant that you were pretty special. When I announced it, I always took a deep breath and drew myself up a little taller, so great was the reputation of the school. And when family or friends asked my father, "Where does Lorraine go to school?" he would reply loudly, "Hunter College, and you know they're not standing out there on corners asking any old body to go there!" We couldn't have been prouder had it been Harvard.

When I got the good news, the whole family called all around to spread the word—here was the first grandchild, niece, cousin to go to college—and to Hunter, no less. It was a fine excuse for a party and for gifts. I was given clothing and some money so that I could go looking like a "college girl." I bought penny loafers, a belt with a cowboy buckle, bobby socks, and jeans, and with the $25 Brotherhood Award that I received at graduation, I went to Fourteenth Street and bought red suede cowboy boots and a huge fake camel-hair wrap coat that had a long scarf that I wound around my neck and threw over my shoulder. I thought I was *très* collegiate.

I made a point of appearing at my old high school one day wearing the red suede boots, jeans with the cowboy belt, a turtleneck sweater, and the great coat. They gasped—the effect I wanted. "This is the way we dress at college," I explained.

I was actually the second person in my family to go to college. My mother's oldest brother, Uncle Buddy, had gone, but he didn't graduate. I was the oldest grandchild, and it was understood that I was to show the way. I graduated, and subsequently so did my sister and a good number of cousins.

"We're Hunter Girls!"

I was amazed when I walked around the Hunter College campus for the first time: the quad, the rock garden, the tennis courts, and the spacious grassy areas. (This was Hunter's "uptown campus" in the Bronx, today the site of Lehman College.) The five of us from the Lincoln Park Honor School or Commerce High School were in awe— "We're actually Hunter girls!"—and we proudly wore our purple-and-white freshman beanies for a whole week.

Our freshman year was Hunter's second year as a coed school. (Hunter had originated in the nineteenth century as a "normal school"—that is, a teacher's college, for women only.) We looked down on those boys who'd been accepted there—accepted, some of us said, because the school so desperately needed boys who didn't mind being called "Hunter boys." But it didn't stop us from shamelessly flirting with those boys, making each of them feel like an Adonis, I'm sure.

On our first day, when we frosh filed into the small auditorium for orientation, we were awed by the appearance of the president of Hunter himself, George Shuster. He made us all feel smart and privileged. But a subsequent speaker introduced some of the cold reality of college. "Look to your left, look to your right," he said. "One of you will not be here next year." His remarks had a sobering effect on me. I made a vow: "I will be one of the ones here next year." I little realized how hard I'd have to work to stay at Hunter.

Surviving—but Barely

I'd failed only one course in high school, trigonometry. I attributed that failure to not being taught properly and to feeling uninterested once I saw that the teacher related only to those students who "got it" right away—Fumio Hagahara and six other math whizzes. I often thought, "Why am I in this course? I didn't ask for it, and I don't need it to graduate." I therefore discounted this failure as not being my fault and faced my freshman year at Hunter ready for success.

But within a week at college, I knew I wasn't ready; high school had not prepared me for academic rigor. I had never written a long composition or a research paper, I had never had to organize my time to complete a volume of work, as there never *was* a volume of work. Although I was well read, I had never had to think or write critically about anything assigned in high school.

By contrast, every class at Hunter demanded reading, writing, and thinking. The professors gave assignments that made me think they were oblivious of my academic load. "Doesn't he know that his course isn't the only one I'm taking?" I'd lament. I took English literature,

Western Civilization, college algebra, German I, and physical education. There was long, hard reading in most of the courses (for which we received free texts). There were midterms and finals—even in Phys Ed. But there was also the ability to cut classes with impunity, unheard-of in high school. Three cuts were allowed in each course, and I figured out how and when to space them to give me time to go to the library and to write last-minute papers.

I spent hours studying, hours in the library, and long, late hours writing term papers—by hand. My mom would wake up at 1:00 or 2:00 a.m. to find me hunched over my books at the kitchen table. "Lorraine, you still up?" she would ask. "Let me fix you some hot chocolate. I'm worried. Are you nearly through?"

I'd lie and say, "Yes, Mama, just another hour, and I'll be done." She didn't believe me, but she was so proud of me, how could I not persevere? I lost half my hair during my freshman year, but I survived academically—with a D+ average.

By the beginning of my sophomore year, I'd settled into a routine. I refused to stay in the student cafeteria beyond my designated time. I never learned to play bid whist or bridge. Once a group of card players desperate for a fourth tried to teach me, but they were soon disgusted with my inability to remember who played what card. "Who cares?" I thought. I slid away quietly after the first game, never to be asked again. I'm glad I never learned those habit-forming games; a few incurable players graduated late or not at all because they'd missed so many classes while playing cards.

Eccentric and Brilliant

Hunter College was one of the toughest and most rewarding challenges I have ever faced. Ninety-eight percent of my teachers there were passionate, eccentric—and brilliant. The chair of the Philosophy Department impressed me because he seemed to know so much about everything. I liked his image, too. He dressed in a slightly careless manner, wearing a tweed jacket with leather elbow patches, just like the college professors in B movies. Because of him, I developed a lasting love for reading about philosophy, especially Eastern philosophy.

Professor Gutekunst taught us "Scientific German" (I was a pre-med major at the time) in a lab where we sang German songs and ate *pfeffer-neusse* at Christmas. I learned I had a knack for dissecting when I worked on a fetal pig in Zoology; I got an A for exposing the brain and spinal cord.

There was Dr. Wheeler, who loved Shakespeare and read us Shakespeare's works with fire and corn. And Dr. Bowden, who read Chaucer with a hesitant, cultivated British accent and who made us memorize the beginning lines of *The Canterbury Tales* in the original Middle English. And Professor Calder, who taught me to love Emily Dickinson's poetry.

Then there was the French teacher who came to lecture in our Humanities course on medieval poetry. He got so worked up that he took off his jacket and revealed that he'd only ironed the collar, cuffs, and front of his shirt. We chalked this up to the delightful eccentricity of a scholar.

One of the best was a music professor, Bruce Prince Joseph, who said he was related to the painter Toulouse-Lautrec. He loved baroque music and played it on the harpsichord. (I had never heard of that instrument before.) His classes met in the auditorium across from a room where I was captive in a required sociology course with a young, self-conscious, abysmally dull teacher. After five minutes of sociology class, my forehead would ache, and after ten minutes, my frontal lobes went dead. So I took all three cuts to go across the hall to sit in the back of the balcony to watch Bruce Prince Joseph teach.

He loved his subject and consciously brought to teaching the techniques and talents of an actor. He'd move around the stage, speak loudly and then whisper for effect. He'd illustrate fugues on the piano and then help you hear the beauty of contrapuntal music on a recording. In his teaching, he exhibited the kind of knowledge and passion that I later tried to incorporate into my work.

And he made my poor sociology teacher look bad. Once when the sociology teacher was late to class, I did an imitation of him in the front of the room. The other students were roaring, and I was on such a roll that when they stopped laughing, I kept on going till I realized he was standing in the doorway. Mumbling, "I'm sorry, very sorry," I slinked to my seat. He didn't hold it against me. I got the C I deserved.

I had a secret crush on Professor Gehren, who taught a survey English course. He always prefaced his discussion of an author's work with biographical tidbits that I found fascinating. I remember getting a B on one paper on which he commented, "You've included *too much* biographical detail." I didn't argue, but I really believed that the lives of the authors were as wonderful as the works—except when we read Wordsworth's "Ode on Intimations of Immortality." Then it was not the man but the work that spoke to me, expressing feelings I intuitively understood but that had never come to my full consciousness.

I understood the entire meaning of this poem, but one day I went up to Professor Gehren after class and asked for an appointment to see him so he could make plain the parts I didn't get. The day of the appointment arrived, and I went into his tiny office. Professor Gehren asked, "What part of Wordsworth's poem don't you understand?" Instantly my eyeglasses steamed up. I snatched them off quickly, and we both went through the charade of interpreting a few lines. I escaped his office, and in order to be able to go to class for the rest of the semester, I pretended the encounter had never happened.

I minored in speech. In one course, called Oral Interpretation of Literature, we had to recite something every session. Sometimes there were assigned texts, sometimes impromptu reading, and sometimes free choice. I remember rehearsing in the bathroom in Gillette Hall for its resonance. One verse I had to present was this:

If thou of fortune be bereft
And of thy store there be but left

Two loaves, sell one and with the dole
Buy hyacinths to feed thy soul.

I was so taken with this verse that I carried a copy of it in my wallet for years and have ever since followed its advice and invested in beauty.

The Deadly 2 Percent

If 98 percent of my teachers at Hunter were magical, there was 2 percent who were not. I probably learned much from the nonmagical 2 percent—about how *not* to teach and motivate students.

In Qualitative Analysis and Quantitative Analysis (two chemistry courses), the professor generally gave out the assignment sheets and then sat on a stool in the front of the room, kibitzing with the Russian twins who were acing the course, watching the rest of the students working and me playing with the centrifuge machine. I hadn't the foggiest notion of what was going on or why it was important, nor did the professor see fit to approach me or offer tutoring. I got two Fs.

There was also a deadly speech teacher. He was so awful that the first student to arrive for class would always start an attendance sheet immediately. That way, if the teacher was fifteen minutes late—the statutory limit for how long students were required to wait—we could leave it on his desk and run out. Sometimes I would stand on the windowsill so that I could see if he was coming across campus. I remember once jumping down from the sill, yelling, "I don't see him. Hurry up, sign the sheet! Fifteen minutes is up. Let's go!" We ran out of class, but unfortunately we chose the very stairs he was coming up and nearly knocked him over. He glared and pointed up to the second floor, and we trudged back to another excruciatingly dull class.

The last nonmagician I remember was in the German Department. Her demeanor was cold and threatening, and she seemed determined to prove that we were not capable of learning her language. We read and translated the novel *Emil und Die Detective* going line by line, snakelike around the room. Of course, all you did each class was try to predict which lines would be yours and focus on translating those lines—forget about appreciating the language or nuances of meaning. The room was lifeless, filled with our dread of her just once deviating from her pattern of snaking around the room. She never did, so I learned nothing and got a C.

Backing into My Life

Recently, after I gave a speech to a group of educators in California, a woman came up to me and said, "This is the first conference I've been to where there's been a black keynoter. It was so good to see you and hear the things you had to say. You told the story of my life ten times over. Thank you." When I hear comments like this one, I can't help thinking, "If someone had told me, when I first started teaching English in the same junior high school I had attended only a few years before, that I would one day be traveling the world talking to people about life in education, I would never have believed it."

The truth is, I did not want to teach. Teaching was a profession I never considered as a teenager. I thought there could be nothing more nerve-racking and thankless than to teach squiggly, noisy kids.

I always thought, however, that my life should be devoted to service to others. Service is what my minister, James H. Robinson, talked about from his pulpit at the Church of the Master in Harlem. I figured that being a missionary doctor in Africa would be just the proper thing to dedicate my life to. It's what my paternal grandfather, Grandpa Ed, had gone off to do, but didn't, sidetracked by wine, women, and the sea. So it fell to me, the eldest grandchild, to become the doctor.

Besides, I thought, the practice of medicine yields such obvious and immediate results: if something is rotten, you cut it out; if a limb is crooked, you straighten it. Teaching? Where are the immediate and obvious results of teaching? Teaching seemed to be a work of faith—an operation done in the dark where the results were rarely visible right away, leaving the doer wondering if she had really done anything at all. So I intended to go to Africa, like Albert Schweitzer, whom I'd read about in my Africa period. I even secretly named myself Lorraine Afrika Williams—L.A.W. seemed like a powerful set of initials (although I never considered becoming a lawyer).

But as I was to learn, you can't outrun your fate. One day in my junior year at Hunter, my counselor (whom I had never seen before) summoned me to her office. I sat on the edge of the chair that she pointed to and tried not to look anxious. She opened my file and said quietly, "So, Lorraine, I see here that you want to be a doctor."

"Oh, yes," I began. "That's what I've always wanted to be." She waited with practiced patience as I ran breathlessly through my Dr. Schweitzer/Africa dream, the sad lapse of Grandpa Ed, and so on.

"Well," she replied when I paused for breath, "I see here that you've received Fs and Ds in Analytical Geometry, Qualitative Analysis, Quantitative Analysis, and any other subject having to do with numbers. What medical school do you think is going to take you with marks like these?"

The fact was that I had never even thought about it. I was at once embarrassed and stunned at the record I had made, and I answered, "I don't know."

She countered with, "I don't know either." But then, more gently, she went on, "But look at all the As and Bs you've gotten in English. Why don't you become an English teacher?"

"Okay," I replied. And so in a millisecond I backed into the work of my life.

Getting My Feet Wet

With this definite purpose in mind, I took the required courses for prospective teachers: Psychology of the Adolescent, History of Education, Education Philosophy, Lesson Planning 101, and Methods of Teaching English in Secondary School. I did well in all the courses. I got an A in Lesson Planning; I remember being particularly proud of a lesson I wrote using Robert Frost's poem "Mending Wall." Finally, I took Student Teaching, my last semester before graduation.

I was assigned to work with Miss Aronoff at Junior High School 82 in the Bronx. She was an old-fashioned teacher in an old-fashioned school, where the teachers ruled. There were silent changes between classes and no crossing the hall to get to your classroom—you had to walk all the way down to the end and make a turn. Of course, candy and gum were not tolerated, let alone violence or crime.

Miss Aronoff was small and sedate; her voice was a well-modulated bark, communicating that she brooked no interference. I watched her from the back of the room, eager to catch her style and sense of command. She followed rigid routines, from spelling and vocabulary words on Monday to tests on Friday, and there was little conversation between her and the kids in class. She spoke, they listened. I wondered whether I could ever maintain that kind of control once I had my own classes to teach.

Two lucky things happened to me that semester. First, Miss Aronoff got sick for two weeks, and instead of hiring a substitute, they illegally let me take her classes. It was a great opportunity for me to practice my teaching skills and be alone and in charge of a class. I carried on as she did and the class behaved well, not because I was Miss Aronoff's clone but because they knew she'd kill them if I reported any disruptions. When she returned, I said, "Everything went well." She looked as if she had expected nothing else.

The second lucky thing was that Mrs. Ischol was there, my old ninth-grade English teacher and librarian. I remembered her fondly for fine-tuning my knowledge of formal grammar and for introducing me to Dickens and repertory theater. She had a great sense of humor. She really liked kids and, when they were bad, would threaten them with ludicrous punishments: "If you don't stop talking while I'm reading to you, I will pull out your pinky nails with a pair of rusty pliers." These weird threats would make the offending students flinch and then laugh, because how could Mrs. Ischol, who so rarely got out of her chair because of her terrible varicose veins, carry out her threats?

While student-teaching at J.H.S. 82, I enjoyed taking time to talk with Mrs. Ischol and learn from her. What a contrast she was to Miss Aronoff! I also had a chance to chat informally for too brief a time with two very young teachers who seemed to be able to teach and control kids with a sense of humor.

I did two demonstration lessons with Miss Aronoff's students for my supervising teacher from Hunter and passed Student Teaching with an A. Unfortunately, I found that the A meant nothing when I encountered my first real class late that first January. Someone should have warned me about what awaited a new teacher straight out of college going into middle school.

A Hundred Dollars for the Summer

During the summer before I graduated from Hunter, however, I had my first real job in education. A college friend of mine, Frances Parker, asked me if I was interested in working as an assistant director of a summer day camp. She gave me the details, and I went to the Seventh Moravian Church, a five-story building in Spanish Harlem, to apply.

I applied and got the job right away. The director showed me the camp. It consisted of a garage with an abandoned car, a first-floor office, a big, open first-floor space for recreation, empty rooms on the other floors—the building even had a bowling alley—and a closet full of play equipment, with ropes, balls of all kinds, bats, and board games all jumbled on shelves. I guess I looked daunted. The director said, "You're in charge of all of this, starting at 12:30 every afternoon. Clear the building every night before you leave, and drop off the keys with the man in the bodega next door. (A bodega is a Spanish-style grocery store.) You'll start tomorrow. I'll be here when you arrive."

"What's my salary for July and August?" I asked. My friend had already told me $100, but I wanted confirmation, and sure enough he said $100. I felt so proud: $100! What a difference that would make in my last semester at Hunter! I could pay the registration fee of $10 and not have to ask my mom for allowance, which was $3.75 a week (down from $5, because Mama was struggling financially). I could even get some clothes for school.

I couldn't wait to get home to tell my mom. I could see her come out of the subway at 161st Street and Amsterdam Avenue, and I was at the door when she came puffing up the five flights of stairs. "Ma, Ma, I've got a job! It pays $100 for the summer. I'm assistant director at the Seventh Moravian summer camp."

After she got settled, I tried to explain the job to her and found I could only repeat the salary, the title "assistant director," a description of the building, and the admonition about clearing it out and giving the key to the bodega man. I realized I had not gotten any real details from the director or a clear job description. I had leapt without looking—not the last time I was to do this.

Thrown in the Pool

The next day I showed up and found the director in his office with his feet propped up on an opened desk drawer. "Hi, Miss Williams," he said. "Here are the keys. Some kids are around. Others will come."

"How many are registered?" I asked.

"It varies," he said. "It depends if their mothers send them. Just keep them busy. Try to keep them on the first floor and out of the street. Oh, and they can't use the bowling alley—I've locked up the balls and pins. Get lunch stuff for them from the bodega next door, and by the way, there should be some kind of closing program for the parents by the end of second week in August." With a final, "Okay, Miss Williams. It's all yours. See you tomorrow," he was gone.

I gathered the kids together. There were about a dozen boys and girls, aged four to twelve, mostly dirty and snotty-nosed, with a dampish smell about them. "Hi," I said. "I'm Miss Williams, the new assistant director."

"Where's Mr. Wilson?" one asked.

I said, "He's gone. Who can tell me what you've done so far this summer?"

"We run around and play," one volunteered.

"Okay, good. What has Mr. Wilson done with you?"

"Oh, he gives us the balls and ropes and games and lets us run around and play."

I said, "Have you gone on any trips?" Like where, they asked. "To the park or the zoo or the aquarium?"

"Nah—we just run around and play. And we're hungry—he didn't give us no lunch."

Ah, the bodega, I remembered. "Wait here," I said. I went next door and got bread, bologna, mayonnaise, and Kool-Aid, and herded the kids into the kitchen. "Sit while I make lunch," I told them. They wriggled ceaselessly while I fixed sandwiches and made Kool-Aid.

That first day, I let them run around and play while I watched and monitored to keep the hitting and punching to a minimum. At five o'clock, I began gathering equipment and clearing the building. Finally I locked the door and gave Pedro the bodega man the key at 5:30. "See you tomorrow!" they yelled as they scattered in all directions home.

I walked to the corner with a straight back as if to show that the day had been a snap, but when I sank into my seat on the bus home I fully realized what I had gotten into. Quitting was not an option: "People aren't handing out $100 jobs, you know, Lorraine. Think." As little as I knew about kids, I knew they needed a program, a structure. But what to do? What to do?

No Structure, No Budget, No Nothing

tried to recall everything that had been done for me when I was a kid in school. By the time I got home, I had worked out the rudiments of a plan. I figured we needed to have a schedule for each day; we needed some projects; we needed to go on some trips; and we needed to have a "show-off program" for the parents in mid-August.

So I wrote a list:

Trip to Central Park
Trip to Bronx Zoo (by subway)
Free play
Lunch
Quiet rainy-day games
Organized group games
Special projects
Finger painting
Paper-bag puppets
Oatmeal container drums
Collages
Seeds planted in small milk containers

Then, we could work up a few songs and dances to oatmeal drums and hand-and-feet rhythm for our mid-August program, and (Yeah! Twenty-Year-Old Assistant Director Forges Ahead—Schedule On Paper!) attach some dates and do it! That was all there was to it. I was so proud.

What I could not anticipate, however, was:

❑   We had no budget: "Use what's here," Mr. Wilson would say. A subway trip? "Let them kids duck under the turnstile."

❑ There was no organization or system for the morning hours, from 8:30 to 12:30. This meant I had to impose order on chaos when I came for the afternoon.

❑ Being effective would mean being aware and in control 150 percent of the time.

❑ The program would become popular, so that twelve kids would turn into twenty.

❑ There were no age restrictions, so older teens (thirteen to fifteen years old) would show up occasionally, creating a whole series of new problems.

One of these unanticipated challenges was figuring out how to keep couples out of the abandoned car and out of the bowling alley when I was on the first floor with the younger kids. Once, I had locked up the building at 5:30, and as I walked toward Madison Avenue, I happened to glance back. I saw through the translucent bathroom windows facing the street the shadows of a boy and girl. I cried aloud, "God!" and ran back to the bodega.

"Pedro, give me the keys, quick! There are two kids in the building." I got in and went straight to the bathroom. I threw the door open. Nobody. I stood back, bent low, and looked under the bottom of the stalls. No feet. But I knew they were in there, so I pushed open one door, a second door, a third door. Of course there they were, both standing on the toilet seat.

"Get out," I yelled. "Get out and don't come back!" They ran out. I locked up the building again, thinking, "Why did I take this job?"

There was a mentally challenged teenaged boy (in those days, we would have said "retarded") who came to hang around. I found him once with a girl in the back seat of the abandoned car. "We ain't done nothing yet," she said. He smiled ruefully and repeated, "Yeah, we ain't done nothing—yet." He looked hurt and disappointed.

"Yes," I replied. "And you're not *going* to do anything. Get out, and don't ever show your faces around here again." They never did.

"We Like Miss Williams"

Soon only kids up to twelve years of age were coming. I taught them manners: "No snatching sandwiches and grabbing cups of Kool-Aid. There is plenty for everyone. If I take you on the bus or train, you are to be quiet, with no running and fighting for seats. Give up the seats to adults. When we go out, you have to be clean." (When necessary, I used paper towels to "wash" them.) "When we go to the zoo, do not put your hands or heads into cages. Stay together, and always stay where I can see you," etc. etc. etc.

After two weeks, the kids would anticipate my coming and run to meet me as I came out of the subway. They broke my watchband by hanging on my arm. I came to look forward to being with them, and apart from the hot teen incidents, the only problem arose when I left them alone on the fifth floor to finish their finger painting: they painted the lower walls pink and purple. It wasn't a bad thing, in fact it was pretty, but I didn't think the Moravian Church people would like it, so the kids had to spend the rest of the afternoon washing the paint off.

At the closing program, Mr. Wilson introduced me, and I told the parents how much I enjoyed being with their children. The children showed their paintings and their potted plants, danced, sang, and told what they liked best about the program. There were three answers: "Miss Williams, the trips, and the lunches."

Before I left, Mr. Wilson gave me $75 and said the other $25 of my salary would be sent to me within a week. I never got it. But I did get invaluable experience that I took to my first real teaching job, five months later.

On Being an Idealist in
a Less-Than-Ideal World

You get what you work for and what you deserve—*sometimes.*

~

Unfortunately, competence isn't always rewarded. But there's still no alternative to being competent!

~

To get on with the work, there are times you have to compromise. But learn the difference between compromising and selling your soul.

~

Good works will be recognized—ultimately. But if you work for the recognition alone, you may be in for a *long* wait.

CHAPTER 5

Believing in Me

RISING ABOVE THE PEOPLE
WHO WOULD DRAG YOU DOWN

Before I graduated from Hunter College, someone told me to send post-cards to junior high schools advising them of my immediate availability to teach. Of course, I sent one off to J.H.S. 82, where I'd just gotten an A in Student Teaching. I got an immediate reply, "Sorry, we have no vacancies." I guess I was naive to imagine they might hire me. There were no adults of color working anywhere in the building, and very few black or brown students.

But when I sent a card to my alma mater, J.H.S. 81, I received a better reply: "We have a job for you as a *per diem* English teacher. Please report on January 26th." The date meant I would miss my college graduation ceremony. But what a thrill—to actually be employed as a teacher! I felt privileged to be back teaching in the same school I had attended; I was actually on the staff with teachers who had been my teachers.

Baptism by Fire

arrived at 7:30 on the morning of January 26 and was given this greeting by a secretary: "Welcome. This is the sign-in book; sign in the time you arrive and the time you leave. Here is your key to your room, 406, and the key to the teachers' lounge and bathroom. And here is the roll book for your homeroom class. Enter attendance and late-nesses in ink, and do not ever erase anything. Remember, your roll book is a legal document." That was the sum total of my orientation.

I found my way to Room 406. It was large and boxy, with a clothing closet with rolling doors on one side, adjacent to the teacher's clothing closet; on the other side was a wall of windows by a book cabinet. There were two doors at the front left and right sides of the room. There were six rows of six desks, each of which was bolted to the floor. The teacher's desk was in the front of the room, and the front wall consisted of blackboards. The room smelled of old books, chalk, and an unidentifiable musty smell.

I opened the windows and doors in hopes of freshening the air. I found a small gray basin and a rag, got some water, and washed the boards. As they dried, I checked the desks and discovered one source of the smells in the room: there were pumpkin and sunflower seed hulls, candy wrappers, and scrunched paper that had held pickles—the kind I had loved so much in the seventh and eighth grades. Later, I decided, I'll have the girls clean out their desks.

On the board I wrote, "Welcome 7–6. I'm Miss Williams, your new homeroom and English teacher." Having received my class program earlier, I knew that I would be teaching English to seventh-, eighth-, and ninth-graders who were at "all levels of intellectual capacity." My own class, 7–6, was considered six steps down in smarts from 7–1, which was the brightest class, but I also taught English to classes 7–11, 7–25, 8–3, and 9–1. I taught six periods a day and had one period of yard patrol and one period for lunch—which, I was to discover, I would have no stomach for.

When the bell rang for the students to come upstairs, I jumped, realizing, "This is it—here they come, ready or not!" As I stood with my back to the board, some girls rushed into the room, stumbling over one another and scrambling for seats; others sauntered in and demanded seats already occupied, or walked around selecting good seats for the anticipated sport of "getting the new teacher."

When the full complement of thirty-six girls had settled into their seats, I drew myself up to my eleventh-grade English teachers Edith Mahoney's erect posture and used my best vocal imitation of veteran Miss Aronoff: "Girls, may I have your attention, please."

They kept talking.

I asked again. Still the conversations continued. I tapped the board with a piece of chalk as Mr. Lindquist, my old high school American History teacher, did. That didn't work either.

Finally, I yelled, "Quiet!" and some were startled into observing my command.

"Now, let me have your attention!" I was still speaking over several girls who proceeded with their conversation.

"I'm your new homeroom and English teacher, and we will be together until June." This quieted a few more.

"Shut up, y'all," said one of the saunterers that I had noticed, a short stocky girl with a round face and mischievous eyes. The class got quiet for a while, and I repeated in a more modulated voice, "I'm Miss Williams and I will be your permanent teacher until June. We're going to learn a lot and have a lot of fun."

The talking started up again before I could continue laying out my plans for them. I decided to put some work on the board, and I asked the girl who had told the class to be quiet, whose name was Doreen Thompson, to give out the grammar texts. She did, slapping each one down and making conversation with her friends while circuiting the room. Doreen, I was to learn, was the class ringleader. She'd intervened to silence her classmates that first morning as a way of asserting her authority among the other girls, as well as to display her power to the new teacher.

Some did the work I assigned completely, some did part of it, and a few did nothing but talk. I felt dismayed and ineffective. That first class of seventh-grade girls nearly drove me out of the profession. Maybe the low point was when Doreen Thompson approached my desk, looked me dead in the eye, and said, "We've had six teachers before you, and we'll have an eighth."

I could not believe her impertinence; in fact, nothing at school or in life had prepared me for the rudeness of this twelve-year-old and her classmates.

I said to her, "I'm not going anywhere. Take your seat," and she shuffled away from my desk, talking to the girls along the route to her seat.

Not About to Quit

My program was a nightmarish one. The only free time I had was lunchtime, and my classes included a daunting array of students—"gifted," average, and those in need of reading assistance. It was, in truth, the program from hell, specially designed to test whether I had it in me to survive and teach or needed to choose another profession.

But the fact is, I've never quit anything. I was the first person in my family to graduate from college, and here I was getting paid a steady salary that enabled me to help my mom and sister. I was not about to quit, even after Doreen came up to my desk one morning and said, "Teacher, what would you do if I hauled off and slapped you?" I said quickly, "I don't know, but I don't suggest that you try it." Doreen went back to her seat, as surprised by my aplomb as I was.

It was the same Doreen Thompson, the class historian and ringleader, whose aim in life seemed to be to scare me away, who actually issued the challenge that made me remain. After lunch sometime during that first Hell Week, she came up from lunch early and knocked on the door.

"Hi, Miss Williams. Can I come in?" she asked in a phony, cheery voice.

"Yes," I said, not really wanting to see her face before I absolutely had to. "What can she want?" I wondered.

"You know," she said matter-of-factly, "our last teacher got pushed into his clothes closet."

"Really?" I said as calmly as I could.

"Twice," she added. "And you wanna know what else we—I mean, some kids—did?" Giving me no time to say no, she went on, "Some kids set fire to papers in his desk. You can see for yourself. Look in the bottom drawer."

I opened the drawer, and papery ashes fluttered up as I shut the drawer quickly. I tried to look unshocked as I thought, "Lord, Lord, what have I gotten myself into? I could be a manager-in-training at Macy's or Gimbel's!"

When I did not give Doreen the appalled reaction she expected, she looked disappointed, but she went on with what I guess she estimated was her ace. "You see that clock up there on the top of the closet? Mr. Franklin, our last teacher, said he wanted us someday to be quiet enough so he could hear the clock tick." With gleeful pride, she concluded, "And he never did hear it."

"Well," I replied firmly, "I am not Mr. Franklin." And I gave her an early version of the "Monroe death stare" that later became famous among my students.

Teaching from Memory

As a twenty-one-year-old novice, I knew nothing about how to teach, despite the education courses I'd taken; I only knew American and English Literature. So I relied on memories of what I'd experienced as a student.

I remembered Miss Dennis teaching me *Julius Caesar* line by line in the eighth grade. I remembered the kindness of Miss Katz in the first grade. I remembered Miss White's attention to me during her lunch duty in the schoolyard when I was in the third grade, and the confirming words she wrote in my autograph book in the sixth grade: "Hitch your wagon to a star; you will go far."

I remembered Mr. Cooper, who'd encouraged me to run for the position of student council secretary, and I remembered Mrs. Graves, who practiced benevolent terror—and created the AEL club to encourage and inspire me and my classmates. Some of the ways of working of each of these teachers I took and amalgamated into my own style.

Little by little, over those first few days of teaching, I discovered ways of taking control in the classroom. I realized that I could not teach the way some teachers do, by writing notes on the blackboard and then explaining the notes orally. (I call this method "Chalk/Talk/Teaching.") Instead, I found that I had to make my blackboard notes and instructions so clear and explicit that the students could understand them and learn directly from them. I would follow this by choosing exercises and readings from the textbook that were so meaningful and clear that students could learn from them with minimal oral explanation. Only in this way, I found, could I establish order while not wasting the students' time, and my own, with Mickey Mouse work.

I also realized that I could not sit down, ever—at least not until one day in the second or third week, when I found six large discarded texts in the bottom of a closet. I piled them on my chair and perched on these, which allowed me to see the whole room.

During lunch, I covered the board with work. When the students returned, I said, "Put your things away in the closet. Take your seats, take out your notebooks, copy the homework, and get started with the work on the board." Like a broken record, I repeated these instructions over and over and over until it wore most of them down.

Occasionally, I found that I was able to impart orally some English knowledge to my students. But each day as I left school, I would put an S.O.S. note in the cute straw basket hanging outside the principal's door. My notes detailed the ridiculous behavior of some of my girls and contained pleas for suggestions and help. The notes were never answered or even acknowledged. Eventually, I stopped writing them and realized that it was up to me to tame the girls.

I began preparing 60 minutes' worth of work for each 45-minute period, so that no student could ever say, "Teacher, I'm finished," and start looking for trouble to get into. I never sat down except on my perch of books on my chair, so that I could watch Doreen and her friends in the Siberian row at the far end of the room.

I never smiled. I wore severe, matronly, nonclinging clothes. I repeated the same phrases ad nauseam: "Come in quietly, take your seat, begin work immediately." I repeated them so often I'd dream them at night—and dream they would one day prove effective.

Once after I'd finally gotten order, during a silent reading period, Doreen came up to the desk with a scrap of paper with the word "orgasm" written on it. "Miss Williams," she asked, "what does this word mean?"

I gasped. "Why, Doreen," I said, "that word has so many consonants I can't even pronounce it. Go home and ask your mother."

After four months, the girls finally understood that I wasn't to be worn down or driven away. I wasn't going anywhere. Somewhere in their little brains, they also realized that they were actually learning English usage, grammar, writing, and literature. Stranger still, they were coming to like the calm and routine of Miss Williams's classroom.

One day, a holy one in memory, I sat on my perch looking over the group and realized that *they were all actually working*. I wanted to weep with joy. "They're doing what I asked!" It was a miracle from God.

By mid-April, they began to take real pride in being good. I could leave the classroom doors open and not be embarrassed by their behavior. They even became an honor class for attendance, punctuality, and behavior. The first time they were recognized as an honor class during the weekly assembly period, they were so shocked they were initially reluctant to stand and receive the applause of their peers and teachers. I had to stand first and motion them with my hand to join me. They finally did so, beaming.

Of course, there were periodic lapses into silly seventh-grade-girl misbehavior, but my daily perseverance, the constant exertion of my will, worked.

No one at home ever knew what I was suffering those first four months. I couldn't talk about my difficulties, but the work took its toll on me. At last, one day in mid-April, I went home and collapsed on the couch. I stayed there for a week, being ministered to by my mother with her home remedies—teas, iron tonics, soups, and specially enriched eggnogs.

When I finally returned to school, Doreen asked, "Where was you? Was you sick? We missed you. We had a lot of subs, and we was even kinda good for them."

The Adjustment Class

Because of my success in instilling discipline, the principal or his assistant changed my teaching program in the middle of my second year. A teacher named Miss Grunfeld had a class of boys in what was called the Adjustment Class. What they were supposed to "adjust" to was socially acceptable behavior. How they were to be made to adjust was left up to the teacher.

Now, the boys behaved well for Miss Grunfeld. I guess any kid would have. She always wore a dour expression; happiness seemed alien to her and joy unknown. Even in the company of her crazy colleagues, who cut up and played pranks during free times in the lounge, she never smiled and rarely spoke. When she did, it was to proclaim that we were the reason education was going to the dogs.

Her special method of controlling the boys remained a mystery to me until one day I rounded a corner as she was lining them up in the hall. She went down the line, and any boy who was out of line in any way got a whack on his funny bone with the sawed-off broomstick she carried.

Now these same boys were transferred to me in the middle of the year—without notice, as I recall. Why? I never determined. One afternoon, they walked, or rather galloped, into my room. Remarkably, each one seemed to be able to gallop in a direction different from that of his peers. It took at least fifteen minutes to get them seated—fifteen minutes of, "Teacher, he hit me," "Teacher, I ain't got no pencil," "Teacher, he took my book."

The quiet demeanor, relentless repetition, and overpreparedness that had worked with my other classes did not work with this crew. I tried putting texts on their desks with papers marking the pages we'd be working on; I tried putting pencils on their desks and explicit instructions on the board. I'd write on the board:

1. Come in quietly.

2. Take your seat.

3. Open the book to the page where the paper is.

4. Do examples 2 and 3.

5. Write answers out in full sentences.

6. Do not talk or get out of your seat.

7. We'll go over this exercise in 15 minutes.

It didn't work. Boys got out of their seats, crossed the room, asked for the hall pass, hid in the clothing closet. One day a boy got on top of the clothing closet and lay down. It was sheer chaos.

I refused to scream. At the end of my first day with Miss Grunfeld's class, she passed me slowly in the checkout room wearing the happiest smirk I had ever seen.

Day after day, the boys cut up. I was humiliated by my ineffectiveness, which was caused by my refusal to hit them; they had become accustomed to being subdued through violence, which I would not practice.

After a week or so, I went down at lunchtime to the principal and said, "I am going home this afternoon if you don't come up to my room."

He answered, "Miss Williams, you wouldn't do that, would you?"

I replied, "If you think I'm joking, just don't come up."

I figured that a new young teacher who had proved herself in a semester with a multi-preparation program (grades seven, eight, and nine, all levels) would not be easy to replace. So the principal and his two assistants came up the first period after lunch and sat in the back of the room with their clipboards. The boys were lambs. They came in, sat down, started work, raised their hands, and learned something.

I was both furious and pleased. "See?" the principal said. "They were as good as gold!"

"Why wouldn't they be," I retorted, "with all of you there?"

"Okay," he said with a sigh. "We'll give them back to their original teacher." I guess, after all, that they didn't want to lose me. And if the principal hadn't given in, I fully intended to leave—to do what, I had no idea.

From that day on, Miss Grunfeld never spoke to me. I couldn't have cared less.

I Didn't Sound Black!

I taught in junior high school for nearly ten years. During that time, I met and married Hank Monroe, and our two wonderful children were born. Finally, after a decade in teaching, I took the exam to be licensed as a high school English teacher. I could have had that license all along had my counselor at Hunter College told me to check the high school box in addition to the junior high school box on the exam application; somehow all the other English majors knew to do this. At any rate, I took the exam and did very well, coming in second on the ranking list, behind number 1 by a fraction of a percent.

The scores were published in a civil service newspaper, and I got a call inviting me to come in for a job interview from the secretary of one of the specialized high schools. I was flattered to be asked. On the appointed date, I put on my interview outfit—navy blue suit, white blouse, pearl necklace and small pearl earrings, and sensible black pumps. I looked professional and felt ready to shine.

When I entered the school, the first person I saw was an African-American man mopping the floor in the lobby. I went up to him and asked, "Are there any other black people working here?"

He said, "You're looking at him." His reply prepared me for the interview.

When I greeted the principal's secretary with the words, "Good morning, I'm Lorraine Monroe. I have a nine o'clock appointment to see the principal," her mouth dropped open and her hairdo nearly became undone. I guess she wanted to say, "You didn't *sound* black on the telephone!"

She went in to the principal and emerged a few minutes later, composed. "He'll see you now," she said with restored cordiality.

I went in and took the proffered seat. The principal was coolly courteous as I answered the routine questions: "What advanced degrees do you have?" "What languages do you speak?" "What is your high school teaching experience?"

Despite the fact that I had been successfully teaching grades seven, eight, and nine for nearly ten years, the principal concluded the conversation with the words, "I'm afraid we can't use you"—just as I'd expected after my talk with the custodian.

I felt disappointed, although I recognized this rejection as racist, not personal. The principal probably wondered, as so many other foolish white people did then and do now, "Can a black teacher teach smart white kids?" I left feeling stupid for hoping and expecting that he would take a black person seriously.

In the Midst of Despair

So in the infinite wisdom of the Board of Education, I was ultimately assigned to Benjamin Franklin High School in East Harlem, one of the worst schools in the city at that time. I accepted the job because I wanted and needed a change.

My experience at Benjamin Franklin High School, a place of light and darkness, consisted of two unforgettable years. Because of the school's history and a pervasive internal and external culture of low expectations and minimal effort, failure was rampant there. The rescue work I saw being attempted was woefully inadequate to the task; the school had simply slipped too far down.

There was a cadre of hardworking, caring teachers and administrators at Benjamin Franklin, but they could not fight the pull of the street and drugs, which were luring inner-city kids away from school, hard work, and hope for the future. And there were too many staff members who regarded their work as just another job rather than a mission. As a result, the school had pockets of excellence but no positive, pervasive organizational hum. Despair fed despair.

Further undermining our efforts was the late-sixties "fuck the establishment" mentality. College kids who were playing at protest and resistance came to the school and tried to lure our students into joining them. I remember teaching one afternoon when a white hand, reaching in from the hallway, found the light switch and switched the lights off. A voice from the other end of the hand said, "Come on out! Come on— fuck school!"

My kids looked at me, wondering how I would respond. I looked at them and said, "Not one of you move. I'm the only one who dismisses this class. These college kids in their overalls, when they're finished playing resistance, will go back over the hill to Columbia. Then one day they'll take off the overalls and join their fathers' firms or their fathers' friends' firms. Raise your hand if your father or his friends work for a firm."

No hands. "Okay, raise your hand if your father or mother is a captain of industry!"

No hands. "Okay, then, let's continue with our essay practice for the Regents."

Nonetheless, some of our kids left school, joined the college kids on the streets, got involved with drugs and early parenthood, and were lost permanently, with no diplomas, no job prospects, and no hope.

Feeling Square

The chaotic atmosphere of the sixties didn't affect the students alone. Shortly before I left Franklin, another teacher invited me and my husband to a Saturday-night party in a loft downtown. I was curious to see the loft living that was then so fashionable, so we went. When we got there, most of the guests were seated in a circle. The first thing I noticed was that some kids from school were there. This threw me, because I never partied with kids at night except at proms or school dances. "Oh, well," I thought, "this is not your party."

The second thing I noticed was that there wasn't any food around. "Where are the noshes?" I wondered. "Maybe this is going to be a cut-to-the-chase party—no appetizers, no hors d'oeuvres, just real food. I can live with that."

People made room in the circle for me and my husband, Hank. There was some small talk about school for a while, but still no food. Finally, the hostess got up. "Oh, food!" I thought. I piped up, "You need any help?"

"No," she said. "No help wanted," and she disappeared behind a beaded curtain. In a moment, she came back with a large peanut butter jar filled with dried leaves. "What is this?" I thought. She began passing the jar around the circle, and people took good-sized pinches. I passed the jar on, as did Hank. I felt really awkward and square, too, as I realized that the dried leaves were, of course, marijuana. We could see the other guests beginning to roll and light up joints.

After the jar went around once, I made an eyebrow motion toward the door to Hank. He picked up on my gesture, and I said, "Gosh, it's later than we thought! We have to go—got to relieve our babysitter." No one in the room bought our story, I'm sure, but they graciously said, "Good night. See you Monday." I think they were glad to see the party poopers leave. We quickly escaped down the freight elevator to the street.

"Can you imagine," I said, "if that place were raided, what we'd look like in the newspapers cuffed, with our heads ducked and faces averted?" I could just image the headlines: "Harlem Educator Arrested in East Village Dope Raid." Whew!

Monday at school, it was as if the party hadn't happened.

There were lots of characters at Franklin, but the elevator operator was the strangest. He had made the elevator into a personal nest with a special chair, a radio, and family photos. He stayed in his nest with the doors shut and only opened them when he felt like it or when he got a request for a ride from one of the faculty members he liked.

Luckily, he liked me. One day he called me over: "Hey, you—new teacher—step here a second." I turned to see him beckoning from the door of the elevator. I went over.

He said, "I been watching you. You're working hard for the kids. I like that. I'm going to teach you my secret knock. You knock like this"—he rapped on the elevator wall, two knocks, three knocks, two knocks— "and I ride you. I'm always in here, but I don't ride everybody, just certain ones—the ones that are polite and what teaches the kids."

"I see," I said.

"Let's see you do it," he urged. I looked around, feeling like a ten-year-old getting the password for the clubhouse. No one was coming, so I practiced rapping on the door: two knocks, three knocks, two knocks.

"You got it."

"Thanks," I said. "Thanks a lot." From then on, I rode the elevator whenever I wanted, to the amazement of some of my older colleagues.

How the Other Half Lives

I taught a small class of older kids, seventeen to nineteen years old, who had not done well previously. It was my task to get them all through the state Regents exam in English. I worked them very hard in test preparation techniques: analyzing questions, intepreting test language, using time efficiently, and eliminating the ridiculous and near-right answers. They were sweet kids who wanted to get out of high school and on with their lives; they all passed.

At Christmastime, I decided to take them to Fifth Avenue to see the store windows, the tree in Rockefeller Plaza, and the famous F.A.O. Schwarz toy store. We went downtown on the subway. They were tense with anticipation; they had never been to that part of New York City, although it was a mere twenty-minute ride from their homes.

As we walked past decorated store windows, they were impressed: "Wow, look at those jewels!" "Look at those fabulous dresses!" We looked at the enormous Rockefeller Center Christmas tree, with its thousands of lights and, beneath it, the gilt statue of Prometheus guarding the rink, where skaters glided around the ice to piped-in music.

Then I said, "Now for our next-to-last treat. There's an unbelievable toy store, F.A.O. Schwarz, that you'll love. But listen, if all ten of us go in at one time, the security guards will have a panic attack. So I'm going to feed you in through the revolving doors two at a time. Spread out, don't cluster, and I'll meet you back at the door in thirty-five minutes."

They gaped in disbelief at the toys in the window. Then we put our plan into effect. "Okay, Maria and Keith, go ahead. The rest of you, wait. Okay, Winston and Rosalia, you're next," until all ten were in. Then I went in. Of course security was having fits—five groups of "colored" kids who obviously weren't going to buy anything.

Somehow we did not adhere to my "Don't Cluster" rule. All eleven of us wound up together watching the massive display of electric trains. After 45 minutes we left, with nothing broken and nothing stolen, the kids smiling broadly, their eyes bright. One kid said, "Ms. Monroe, did you see the prices of some of those toys? Who could buy them?"

"Some people do," I said. "One day," I thought, "you might be one of those people."

Finally, we went to Blum's of San Francisco, a fancy ice cream parlor. The kids were wonderfully unselfconscious by then, but at a table near our group sat a (white) woman I had known for years. I saw her looking at me with the pleading look that black people see on the faces of some whites whom they know from school or work. The look tells you that they don't want you to recognize them or to acknowledge that they know you, a person of color. I responded by ignoring her and never speaking of it subsequently.

After two years at Benjamin Franklin, when the opportunity arose for me to go to a new school in the Bronx, I jumped at it. As you'll see, it opened up a whole new chapter in my career and my life.

On Teaching and Learning

What a teacher feels and thinks about the children in front of her makes all the difference in how much those children learn.

∼

When a teacher demonstrates sincerity and decisiveness in the classroom, the children will unconsciously give her permission to teach them. And without that permission, learning won't happen.

∼

A teacher who keeps teaching the same things in the same way slowly but surely dies in front of her students.

∼

Designating a few kids as gifted and talented brings out all their gifts and talents. In education, elitism works.

∼

Race, ethnicity, and poverty are poor excuses for low expectations.

CHAPTER 6

I'm an Idea Whose Time Has Come"

BECOMING A LEADER

In 1970, my principal was moving to a new school, Adlai E. Stevenson High School in the Bronx. Technically, I wasn't eligible to join him, but I was chosen to go anyway—to meet a racial quota, I think. My being chosen to go to Stevenson was a gift from God. The move changed my destiny, because it was at Stevenson that I first had the opportunity to work in a leadership role in a school.

I went, of course, as an English teacher. It was the work I had done for years, had become quite good at, and had truly grown to love. The five English classes I taught each day were a continual challenge and joy to me. I knew and loved my subject, and I'd found I was able to get many of my students to love it as I did.

The autonomy of teaching was enjoyable for me; in my classroom, I was the queen, and I liked that feeling. I also liked seeing my students change and grow as a result of my work with them. Most of all, I loved to hear students groan at the sound of the bell signaling the end of my class period, while we were in the midst of a scene from *Hamlet* or studying the Latin and Greek roots of English vocabulary. I loved teaching.

That first September at Stevenson, Ben Lubell, the English Department chairman, asked me to serve as assistant chairman for the department. I said yes, but a chance walk with another English teacher, Cathy Tierney, through the faculty cafeteria, past the assistant principal, changed that. The assistant principal, John McNiff, stopped us and asked if we'd like to be girls' deans.

We asked, "What do deans do?"

He said, "It's an interesting job—you talk to girls who are having behavior problems." Cathy and I looked at each other and said, "Why not?"

I said, "How is Ben Lubell going to take it? I just told him I'd be his assistant."

McNiff said, "Just tell him you've changed your mind." I felt bad, but for no reason I could give even now, I knew the change was the right one.

When I told Ben my decision, he said, "Go ahead, but you're making a mistake. You'll be dealing with the underbelly of the school. You'll come crawling back, begging me to take you back."

I just might have changed my mind if he hadn't used the words "crawling" and "begging."

What a great choice I made. As the girls' dean for four years, I met all kinds of girls with all kinds of problems, and I met their problem mothers and fathers and stepfathers, too. I learned to talk to crying girls and crying mamas, cursing girls and cursing mamas, and prejudiced mamas. There were the white ones who ranted, "I hate all black bastards—not you, the *other* black bastards!" And there were the black ones who moaned, "You don't *know* how hard it is to be black!"

I learned how to fend off drunken lecherous stepfathers who would come to get their stepdaughters out of school early for "doctors' appointments." I learned that the parents of troubled girls are almost always equally troubled, and I wound up counseling them and referring them for help with their psychological and emotional problems.

I learned that girls who say "Fuck you" to the teacher in front of a class of thirty usually are pussycats in a one-on-one conversation. And

I learned that some teachers bait kids and paint them into corners, forcing the kids to curse or act out so as not to lose face in front of their peers.

Above all, I learned that if I shut up and listened and let people who were angry or frustrated talk or yell themselves into calm, they would often reveal to me how to help them, even if only as an ear or shoulder.

I did this work with Cathy Tierney for four years. We worked day in and day out, only taking some time off for theater and lunch to revitalize ourselves for dealing with the miseries that humans are subject to: poverty, psychological and sexual abuse, hopelessness, and abandonment.

Don't Back Down When You're Right!

Sometime during these four years, my principal, Leonard F. Littwin, called me into his office and said, "Lorraine, I think you would make a good principal." I said to him, "Me, a principal? You gotta be crazy to be a principal!"

He looked shocked, and I quickly added, "I don't mean you, but the others."

I left his office, but Mr. Littwin had planted the seed. I had been going to school to get an M.A. in English literature at Hunter and I was nearly finished with it. I only had to do a course or two and write my thesis on Marlowe's *Richard III*. I'd been thinking that I might want to teach college English one day.

But now I began to seriously consider school administration as a career choice. While working as a dean, I'd watched the principal and the assistant principals working each day, and I'd decided that I could handle most of the problems they tackled as well as they did—and in some cases, better. I could see, too, that having the ability to set policies for a school and to train teachers in working effectively with students could be a powerful force for improving education. I began to think that maybe being a principal was part of my destiny after all.

Driven by the same inner prompting that had sent me to J.H.S. 81 and to Ben Franklin and to the dean's office, I began taking supervision and administration courses at Bank Street College.

In time, I earned a master of science degree in school administration from Bank Street, taking as many as fifteen credits in a single semester to complete the degree. I left the dean's office at Stevenson, taught English for two years, and began longing for a job as a school administrator.

I even applied to be principal at an Upper West Side junior high school. When I was interviewed, the chief personnel officer asked me why I thought I could be an administrator with so little administrative experience. I replied, rather brashly, "Because I'm an idea whose time has come!" Thinking back, I can see what I meant. I felt ready to assume leadership. Through practice and observation, I'd amassed decision-making skills and knowledge of how to deal with all kinds of people, including angry parents, incompetent teachers, recalcitrant kids, and bureaucrats from the Board of Ed. And I certainly had the self-confidence for the job—or *chutzpah*, as we call it in New York.

But I guess my time hadn't come yet: I didn't get that job. But my principal got wind of my applying outside, and he began asking his superintendent to approve the budget for a third assistant principal line, hoping to promote me to that position. Unfortunately, she denied his requests.

As luck would have it, however, at the end of the summer of 1979, when I returned to Stevenson, an assistant principal had to suddenly go away for his wife's health. Mr. Littwin asked me to take the spot. All my papers were in order, and I got my first bona fide administration job in a school of 4,800 kids.

One of the first lessons I learned in this job was not to back down when you are right. My very first memo, outlining procedures to be followed in some mundane matter, took me hours to write. After it was distributed, it was immediately challenged by an angry teacher who came into my office and announced, "I just read your memo, and I don't like it. I'm giving you fifteen minutes to get on the loudspeaker and rescind it." He turned on his heel and left the office.

A bit shaken, I reread the memo, and I still thought it was pretty good. When fifteen minutes had elapsed, my phone rang. It was the angry teacher. "Well," he said, "your fifteen minutes are up."

"Listen," I replied, "I'm not changing a word of it. Do what you think you have to do." I never heard a word from him again. Ultimately, he lost his teaching license for other bizarre behavior.

I learned, too, that the personal beliefs and prejudices people harbor often dictate their behavior. As supervisor of the college counseling office, I called in the school's college adviser for a strategy session. "I want to crack the Ivy League colleges with this year's senior class," I told her.

She was incredulous. "What do you mean, crack the Ivies with these kids? My own son didn't go to an Ivy League school!" She didn't stay long. Two young eager-beaver maniacs took her place—and sure enough, we cracked the Ivies.

And early on, I learned that nothing is more important than being competent. When I first got the job as assistant principal, one of our counselors went in to the principal and declared, "I know why you chose Lorraine for the job."

"Really! Why?"

"Because she's black."

"Wrong," Mr. Littwin replied. "I chose her because she's competent. Now, leave my office."

I can't say enough about the leadership lessons I learned from Leonard Littwin. As the saying goes, he "ran a tight ship." In Mr. Littwin's view, for a school of 4,800 students to run smoothly, the principal, the assistant principals, and the teachers had to meet and talk frequently in order to ensure that everyone was clear about the mission and philosophy of the school. I've carried out this approach in my own schools ever since.

Mr. Littwin also taught me the importance of observation. He took me around the school to sit in on classes with him, and after each class he would ask me, "Lorraine, tell me what you saw in there. How would you advise this teacher? What is she doing right? What could she do better?" I learned from Mr. Littwin that it's impossible to run any organization from behind a desk in an office. You've got to walk around, watch people work, schmooze with everyone, and make yourself visible. It's the only way to really know what's going on and to have a true impact on the operation.

Working as an assistant principal for Leonard Littwin was the best preparation for leadership I could have had.

Challenge Accepted

I remember distinctly the late-summer phone call I got at our summer cabin in upstate New York from Superintendent Robert Folchi asking me whether I'd be interested in taking a principalship. It was the second such call I'd gotten. I'd refused the first time, feeling I wasn't ready. This time I said yes without hesitation, saying to myself, "They're not going to keep asking you, foolish woman!"

After I said yes, I asked what high school. He said, "Taft High School. It's in the Bronx near the Grand Concourse on 172nd Street."

I didn't know the Bronx except for J.H.S. 82, the Bronx Zoo, Union Avenue, where my relatives lived for decades, and Stevenson, which I'd driven to via the Cross Bronx Expressway for nearly ten years. I certainly knew nothing about Taft.

"Then you accept?" he asked.

"Yes," I said.

"Good. Meet me tomorrow at my office and we'll talk."

To my chagrin, no one was at home to share this news with. Hank, my husband, and the kids were out on a long run. I walked outside and looked up and down the road, then went back to the front porch and paced. Why did they have to be out so long? Wow! Principal of a high school. What possibilities! I went upstairs and wrote a list of things I wanted at Taft, now that it would be *my* high school:

1. Start by making Taft a quiet, orderly school.

2. Meet with staff to plan, organize, and *dream* the school together.

3. Look at the curriculum. Figure out who should teach what to whom in order to ensure academic rigor in every course.

4. Prepare our smartest kids to get into the best colleges in the country.

5. Expand the gym program to include more than just a few sports.

6. Above all, honor innovation, creativity, and hard work.

Soon the kids and Hank returned. I was jumping up and down. "Guess what?"

"What is it?" they asked, seeing my anxiety. I blurted out, "You're looking at the new principal of Taft High School in the Bronx. I got a call about an hour ago from Mr. Folchi, the superintendent. I'm so excited!"

"Wow!" the kids said.

"Really, hon?" Hank said. "That's great."

"Do you think we could just drive by and see what it looks like?" I asked. Hank agreed. We drove down into the city, got off the Cross Bronx Expressway at Jerome Avenue, took the Grand Concourse, and somehow kept missing the street that would get us to the school. Not until I'd leaned out of the car window to ask directions several times did we get the right street.

On that hot August night, the neighborhood was as lively as midday. Children were running, playing, and riding bikes and tricycles in the streets and alleys. Men and women were sitting on stoops chatting. The older men sat around card tables under the streetlamps playing cards or dominoes, and the teenagers lounged on parked cars, talking and neck-ing to the accompaniment of loud rock-and-roll. Everyone was outside, escaping the heat of the tiny apartments. It was a scene straight out of my Harlem childhood.

The school loomed up castle-like on a hill, taking up two whole blocks. We drove around it three times, and Hank said, "It looks awfully big, Lorraine. Do you think you can handle it?"

"Of course," I replied with confidence born of ignorance.

"Sure she can!" the kids yelled as we all peered through the windows like lost tourists who'd suddenly found one of the Seven Wonders of the World. But we drove home in utter silence, each of us wondering about the enormous thing I had so recently said yes to.

Strangely, I slept well that night, and I awoke the next morning firm in my commitment to the new position. As we'd arranged, I visited the office of Superintendent Robert Folchi. He was a tall, brooding man who resembled the actor Abe Vigoda, with large, dark, saturnine eyes that could beam benevolently one minute and flash anger the next. He greeted me pleasantly, however. "Congratulations, Ms. Principal. I'm glad you accepted. Lennie said you're good."

Lennie was Mr. Littwin. I said, "Oh, my gosh, I didn't call to tell him!"

"He knows," he said. "Who do you think recommended you? Now to business," he continued. "Ms. Pulitzer, the former principal, called a few days ago to inform me that she was retiring. Let me tell you about the school. There's low student achievement, chaos in the halls, low staff morale, and some trouble with the union. Sy Duchan, one of my assistants, will take you to the school to show you around and answer any questions you may have. Congratulations and good luck."

I rose and shook his hand. "Thank you for this opportunity, Mr Folchi," I said, and I went to find Sy Duchan, a tall man with a sardonic, been-around-the-block-a-few-times air about him. "Hello there, Lorraine. I'll take you up to the school so you can look around."

As we drove, he told me, "There are about 3,200 kids on register. You have eleven assistant principals. You might want to call them or at least call the two first-floor administrators. You have three days before school opens for the kids." That wasn't much time. But for a while, I'd been planning what I'd do when the opportunity to run a school came my way, so I wasn't daunted. As for the student population, 3,200 kids was an average-sized school for that time.

After we entered my office, he said, "Sit in the principal's chair and see how it feels." I did—I felt nothing. Then he sat and said, "Walk around the building and I'll wait here for you." There were four floors. I didn't use the elevator; I walked from floor to floor and peered in at classrooms, mostly unpainted, with window shades missing or torn in most of the rooms. The gyms were, at best, adequate. The auditorium had a balcony and a good-sized stage. The lobby had a marble staircase that led to the second floor.

There was something old and grand about this school that had once been something of an educational gem—an alternative to the Bronx High School of Science, one of New York's elite, specialized schools for the brightest youngsters, especially those interested in science careers. Taft had once attracted kids from the Bronx who might have gone to Bronx Science but chose instead to attend their neighborhood high school.

I came back down to meet Sy. "What do you think?"

"I think I'll like it."

"Okay. By the way," he said as we drove back to the superintendent's office to get phone numbers, "you have your own private bathroom, down the hall from your office, and you have a sink in your clothing closet." Imagine that—what a perk! I could make tea whenever I wanted. The private bathroom turned out to be a dubious perk. Since everyone could see when I left my office to head down the hall toward the bathroom, the trip to the bathroom became an opportunity for staff members to waylay me, saying, "Can I tell you my latest idea? It'll just take a minute." Naturally, it always took more than a minute. Worse yet, there were those who would say, "Oh, are you going to the rest room? Fine, I'll just wait out here and we can talk when you come out"!

Of course, it was better than going to the main bathroom. If I did that, staff members could follow me right in and talk my ear off while I washed my hands. Make no mistake, being a principal is intense work. It got to the point where, on many days, I never ate lunch and never went to the bathroom; I was that busy.

Anyway, to get back to my early days at Taft: Sy had told me, "Martin is one of your first-floor assistant principals, and Peter Engel is the other." By mistake, I called Earl Martin, a dean and shop teacher, and said, "Hello, this is Lorraine Monroe calling. I'm the new principal of Taft, and I'd like to meet with you tomorrow to discuss some plans for the year."

"Who? What? Wow! You're the new principal?"

"Yes."

"Well, that's great news, except I'm not the Martin you want. You want Dr. Calvin Martin. Wow! Congratulations."

I really hadn't wanted the staff to know about me just yet, but I'm sure Earl called some people who called some people . . . so by the time school opened, the entire staff was well aware that a new principal was in place. But I got both Dr. Martin and Peter Engel, and we arranged to meet early the next day.

Some Rules Are Not Negotiable

They laid out for me that next morning the basic problems in the school: not surprisingly, they included lack of discipline, low staff morale, and some poor teachers. Taft had deteriorated to the point where the school was basically out of adult control. There were frequent fights among students, and many of the kids skipped classes with impunity, lounging on the outside steps or on parked cars or hanging around the cafeteria for hours at a time. Some students were doing so little work that there were seventeen-year-olds who had accumulated just five credits out of a total forty-two needed for a diploma.

Above all, the teacher's union would be a major headache for anyone in the principal's role at Taft. Apparently Mr. Folchi had forgotten to tell me how much trouble the union really was. They'd filed almost a hundred grievances in the previous year, tying the principal up with hearings. I think that many of these grievances were motivated by the frustration the teachers felt over how the school was run. This was their way of harassing an administration that was ineffectual in supporting them as educators. Meanwhile, as the teachers and administrators battled one another, kids were running up and down the halls and playing their boom boxes during class.

Having been clued in by Duchan about the strengths and weaknesses of each of my first-floor AP's, I asked each to submit a list to me the next day detailing their duties and responsibilities. I also asked Artie Sievert, my former chief security officer at Stevenson, to meet me at Taft the next day. I realized that our first task was to restore order at the school, and I knew that Artie was a master at organizing security and schedules.

I chose Peter Engel—a great detail-oriented, no-nonsense, get-it-done man—to take over the secretaries, discipline, and guidance, areas that I knew can make or break a school. He met with Artie, who told him how we had managed security and discipline at Stevenson. Peter Engel made the same system work for us at Taft, operating hand in hand with Gerry Bell, our chief dean of security. Dr. Martin was assigned other administrative tasks, which both Engel and I assisted him with until he retired a year or two later.

Most crucially, we established a set of non-negotiable rules, much like the ones I later used at the Frederick Douglass Academy. Just as we had at Stevenson, we had deans on floor patrol. Prior to my coming, the deans sat in offices talking to kids one on one while chaos reigned in the halls. When I met with the deans the first day they came back after Labor Day and explained what the deans' position now entailed—the active clearing of halls and bathrooms, even locking some bathrooms that had become student hangouts—they balked: "This is not how we used to do it. This is not what we signed up for when we applied for the dean's job."

"Well, this is what it is now," I said. "It's all right if you don't want to do it, but understand that you'll then go back to teaching five classes a day, as well as having a homeroom and a period of hall patrol." Without exception they all accepted the new system. One said, "I guess I'd better get my sneakers out."

Every August, a day is set aside for all New York City high school administrators to meet. That year, I attended my first such meeting. I remember walking out of the 66th Street and Broadway subway stop in a dreamlike state, taking the long walk to Martin Luther King, Jr., High School through Lincoln Center Plaza and finally entering the auditorium to find my team—the group of assistant principals, including Engel and Martin, who would be seminal to the changes I had planned since that day Superintendent Folchi called. They greeted me with warm welcomes and gentle looks.

When I was introduced to the entire gathering of administrators as the new interim acting principal of Taft, there was polite applause. They all knew more than I did about what Taft was really like, and there was a sense of "Does she know what she's gotten into?"

At the morning session we were urged by New York City Schools Chancellor Dr. Frank Macchiarola, High Schools Head Nathan Quiñones, and other dignitaries to "Do more with less!" and "Make this a great year!" Then the administrators met in small groups with those doing the same jobs at various schools. Later we went back to our respective schools for planning sessions.

Our Taft afternoon session with my assistants was fruitful. I laid out the new job descriptions for Engel and Martin. Engel described the new security and discipline procedures, and I asked the group, "Based on your experience here, what is the most important issue to be addressed first?"

"Order in the halls," they all agreed. "The kids are out of control."

"All the kids?" I asked.

"No, but lots—enough to make effective teaching real hard."

"What else?" I continued.

"The students don't come prepared to work," someone complained. "They don't bring books, pens, pencils, or notebooks. They walk in with nothing, both hands swinging free. They're not motivated to achieve, they don't want to learn—that's all there is to it."

"Well," I offered, "suppose we see how the new deaning works. And would you look at these rules and regulations I've drafted? Can we all agree to live by them?"

I showed them the twelve non-negotiables: Attend school daily, come on time, bring equipment for learning, don't fight or vandalize, and so on. These were the same rules we'd used at Stevenson, and the group agreed they were good.

One chairman said, "I like the rule about equipment for learning, but I don't think we can get these kids to bring large notebooks to school. They might bring assignment books, but—"

I interrupted. "Oh, they'll bring them, because you're all going to demand it in each of your departments. I'll say it on the loudspeaker, and it'll be in the rules, which we'll distribute on Day One. We'll saturate them with these regulations. They know that kids are supposed to come to school with a notebook and that serious school requires this. If we don't ask for it, we won't get it."

"I still don't see how we're going to enforce it," he persisted.

"We won't let them in the building without their notebooks!" I replied.

"That's illegal," he protested.

I stood my ground. "So?"

He retreated. "Okay, okay, but kids need lead time. You just can't spring it on them."

"You're right. We'll give them till the third day of school."

There was one more objection. "What about some of our poor kids? We have lots of kids who are on welfare. What about them?"

I had a response for that, too. "First of all, kids at Taft are like kids everywhere in America—they see ads starting in August about back-to-school supplies, and so do their parents. They know they need this stuff.

And most of them get the latest sneakers, hats, clothes. They can afford a three-dollar notebook. But on the outside chance some kids really can't, I'll keep a dozen in my closet, which we can very discreetly give to individual kids."

The first day of the full staff's returning, I stood outside my door and introduced myself to the secretaries as they came in. "Good morning. I'm Ms. Monroe, the new principal."

The first to arrive said, "Great! You must be the new secretary we were expecting." A second one responded to my greeting with "Welcome! So you're the new paraprofessional!"

"No," I patiently explained, "I'm your new principal."

I got used to people not expecting a black woman to be principal of a high school. Some time later, the school doctor asked me as I was walking down the hall, "Excuse me, miss, would you open the medical room for me? Do you have the keys?"

"Yes," I responded. And as I opened the door, he commented, "Say, you know you're kinda cute for an aide!"

At our first faculty meeting, many of the teachers sat far back in the last rows of the auditorium. I greeted the group: "Good morning! Please move forward. No one is to sit behind Row L." A good number moved forward, and I moved and spoke from row I. Subsequently this became the rule: No one sits behind Row L.

I greeted them, told them my background, and told them I required two things from them: "You are to plan, and you are to be *magic*."

I caught a few puzzled looks at that. Magic? I explained: Every teacher needs to find a way to use his special gifts, talents, and style to help students catch the teacher's passion for the subject. When I observe a lackluster, boring teacher, I'll often ask him, "How did you choose your major in college? And why did you decide to teach that subject?" The answer is generally, "I always loved history, or music, or math, or biology." "Then," I'd say, "make your students know how and why you came to love it. Communicate the passion!" That's what I call magic.

My message to the teachers continued: "I know many of you are concerned about discipline and order in the halls. We have a plan for handling this, and Mr. Engel will speak to you about it. Once classes start, I will be around often to observe your magic and to see your plans in action. As you'll find, I love to observe. Don't worry, I am not out to get you. I am out to help you to be better teachers so that our kids can learn better. I look forward to this being a wonderful year. Good luck, and I'm very pleased to have been selected your principal."

Setting the Tone

The first day that the kids returned went smoothly as planned. Kids got their programs, and got orientation in homeroom, where they heard about the new rules. The notebook regulation was emphasized. After the kids were dismissed, staff remained to do the final get-ready things, and the counselors straightened out the program glitches.

The next day, there was a full day of school. Every teacher reminded his/her class about the notebook requirement. And the students, surprised to see staff in the halls and the principal visiting classrooms, went to class rapidly.

I also instituted something we had had at Stevenson, a mandated Do-Now—an exercise requiring students to get to work on a three- to four-minute assignment that either spiraled back to past work or prompted thinking and writing about the work of the period. This made coming into the room immediately a must, since the Do-Now was gone over or checked and collected. When students asked, "Does this count?" we answered with an emphatic "Yes."

This combination of deans and teachers in the halls and the Do-Now giving the additional incentive for getting to class on time fulfilled one of my edicts: "Two minutes into every class period, I want to look down the hall from my office and see space."

The staff was elated at the new quiet and order. One teacher said, "This is the first time in years that I've dared to use the stairs." The smiles on lots of staff faces at three o'clock made me, the administrators, and the deans feel very good. Most of the students liked the new school environment, too. They enjoyed coming to a school that didn't replicate the chaos and danger they found on the streets. Having a safe haven from the madness of their neighborhood lives was something they welcomed.

Of course, there were still some kids with problems that couldn't be solved by magic teachers who planned or by deans who patrolled— problems such as being an eighteen-year-old ninth-grader with just six credits toward a graduation requirement of forty-two credits. I asked my deans to give me a list of the names of the twelve most difficult kids; they all had problems like this.

I reviewed all of their records and had the counselors send for their parents to see me with their kids, most of whom were boys. When I confronted the kid and the parents with their academic record, they appeared shocked. Why, I don't know, because the records indicated that most of these kids had been trouble since kindergarten. Often the counselor had noted high absenteeism, cutting classes, failing grades, fighting, and confrontations with teachers and other adults. Under the previous regime, attempts to improve matters had failed: these students had been counseled, held back, transferred, and referred to professionals—all to no avail.

Some mothers (fathers never came) would cry, some would get angry at the boy and shout threats and recriminations: "See there! Now you've done it! I'm tired of you and your ways! Throw him out, I don't care!" I always felt deeply sorry for these women who had long ago lost control of their boys and who were generally overwhelmed by poverty, lack of education, and lots of kids, for whom this one was no help or good example.

I always let the crying, cursing, and accusations die down before I would say, "Look, at his present rate of progress, he will be thirty-eight years old before he graduates. It is not productive for him to stay here, but there are other programs that can assist him in either getting a GED or some job skills. Why don't both of you go with his counselor, who will explain to you the various choices?"

The mothers were pleased, especially when I said, "I never put a kid out to nowhere. There are always options and alternatives." For students who were sixteen or seventeen years old, we recast a program that had been a kind of holding operation for kids who were not doing well but who were coming to class every day and obeying school rules. We gave them classes to prepare for the GED (high school equivalency) test in the morning, and in the afternoon they went to job sites and internships. This worked nicely.

Disarming the Opposition

It takes time to turn a troubled institution around, and at a school like Taft, with a long history of problems, this wasn't easy to change. But during the first few weeks of my time there, we managed to send a clear signal to teachers, other staff, parents, and students that a new tone was being set—one with an emphasis on self-respect, discipline, and quality education. Little by little, the whole school community got the idea, and got involved.

Even before I arrived, I'd been warned about two potential obstacles to my plans for change. One was the local chapter of the teachers' union, the United Federation of Teachers (UFT), which I'll talk about in the next chapter. The other was the custodian. In my previous career, all of the custodians I'd known were great, hardworking guys. They kept the school clean and did what was asked of them regarding building maintenance. But I had been warned by the staff that the custodian at Taft—a Mr. Ford—was terrible. And in the New York City school system, custodians have significant freedom in controlling their own work. At that time, it was hard for a principal to force a custodian to do anything he didn't want to do. (Technically, the principal was required to rate the custodian's work, but she did not supervise him.) In effect, the principal could only make requests, not give orders. So I decided I'd pay careful attention to making sure my relationship with Mr. Ford was a positive one.

Several weeks passed before I met the custodian, but during that time I found his crew to be highly efficient, which greatly reduced my concerns. Finally, one day, a slightly disheveled man a little past middle age shuffled through my office door.

"So you're Ms. Monroe, the new principal."

"I am."

"I'm Ford, the custodial engineer."

I stuck out my hand and said, "I'm pleased to meet you. Your men have done a fine job at getting the building ready for the kids. Thanks."

He straightened up and looked at me curiously. "You seem okay," he commented. "That other one—that other principal, the bitch!—she rated me Unsatisfactory! I wouldn't do a thing for her—*nothing*. Me, Unsatisfactory!"

I said nothing. Ford continued, "I *might* do some things for *you*, but for her, nothing! What color do you like?"

"Yellow," I replied.

"Yellow," he repeated as he left the office.

A few days later, I took a baker's dozen doughnuts down to his office, where I found him deep in conversation with a visiting custodian. "Sorry to interrupt," I said. "This is for you and your men," and I left.

In a few weeks, lo and behold, Ford's men began painting some of our first-floor walls—bright yellow, of course. This despite the fact that I'd been informed, in no uncertain terms, "My men don't paint. Painters come from Central"—that is, the central school board—"and there are only seven painters left in the whole city."

A simple thing like painting is no simple matter in the New York schools. In fact, I was told that Taft High School had not been painted for *twenty-seven years*. Ford did a partial job, but then he retired. He was replaced by an interim custodian. This new man came in, introduced himself, and asked me, "Would you like your office painted?"

"Yes!"

"What color?"

"Yellow," I replied again. His men did it over a weekend.

I guess the custodians were cooperative with me because I liked them and talked to them. Like anyone else, they appreciated being treated with courtesy and respect, and they responded in kind. More important, they appreciated the sense of order and discipline we developed in the school. As vandalism fell, the custodians found that they did not have to spend a lot of time and money on repetitive repairs. They appreciated that, and so they responded quickly to my requests for repairs.

Creating a sense of safety and order was our most important accomplishment during my early days at Taft. Order is crucial to productive work of any kind, including education, but especially in a troubled neighborhood like the Bronx. For most of our kids, school was the only predictable, stable element in their lives. Keeping it secure was vital to their psychological well-being. So we used techniques like hall sweeps (clearing the halls at unexpected times), surprise appearances by staff in unlikely places, and adopt-a-kid programs (choosing a troubled kid to watch and counsel) to prevent violence and foster a sense that the dean, the teacher, or the security guard could also be a counselor and friend.

Most kids, I'd found, hate violence, especially in school. They want their school to be a place where they can drop their façades and the shells of toughness that they need to shield them in their tough neighborhoods. If the street is crazy and chaotic, home is crazy and chaotic, and school is crazy and chaotic too, then kids have no choice but to behave in crazy, chaotic ways—or to turn to gangs to give them the structure, security, and discipline they crave. Most kids in gangs are scared. School has to free them from their fear. Kids want to learn and have fun at school—they don't want school to mirror the street. (I used to tell the students in assemblies, "This is not the street. What goes down in the street doesn't go down in here.") They know that school should be a corny, different place and that's exactly what I had planned to create: a corny, different place.

If kids can have one place in their daily lives where there is order and stability and where worthwhile activities are going on, then there is a high possibility that their lives can be transformed for the better. Our first step at Taft was to make it such a place.

On Leadership (I)

To become an excellent leader, start as an excellent follower.

~

Becoming a leader is an act of self-invention. *Imagine* yourself as a leader; act as if you are a leader until you actually become one.

~

When you undertake leadership, people will challenge and attack you. Just make sure you win your *first* battle, and the others will come easier.

~

The toughest leadership challenge: To inherit something good and not *mess with it!*

~

The real leader is a servant of the people she leads.

CHAPTER 7

The Hum of Excellence"

INSISTING ON QUALITY

I knew that to increase student achievement, we first had to establish order. Christ, Buddha, and Moses could not have taught or led in chaos. But it was a startling revelation to me that once order was obtained, some of the same teachers who had complained, "I would be a better teacher if the kids came promptly and the halls were quiet," still didn't teach!

Some of them hadn't the foggiest notion of how to plan a class with a beginning, a middle, and an end or how to involve and interest kids. And many were used to a system in which there were few incentives for teaching well. It came to my ears that one teacher who had a class of thirty-four students in early September bragged to his colleagues, "I never complain about oversized classes, because when I finish my opening remarks by mid-September, the class is always down to around twenty." I vowed that teachers at Taft would no longer brag about driving students away with boredom!

Leading by Observing

I had learned from Leonard Littwin, my excellent mentor at Stevenson, that classroom observation is the principal's most important method for improving school tone and student achievement. More broadly, I'd realized that being everywhere around the building, observing, listening, and schmoozing with everybody were serious acts of leadership. In business, they call it MBWA: Managing by Walking Around. I call it a key part of the Monroe Doctrine.

So, as principal, I developed a routine. In September, I visited every teacher informally several times, popping into each room to see what was happening. What was on the blackboard—was there a Do-Now? Was there an Aim, describing the purpose of that day's lesson? Was there a homework assignment? Did the wall decorations reflect the subject being taught? Were the students engaged? Did the teacher seem prepared? Was he or she standing, reflecting energy and involvement? Was the classroom alive?

I sent "love notes" to the teachers who seemed to be on track and memos to those who needed suggestions or a nudge. It was during these September visits that I got to know who the stars were, who the well-meaning strugglers were, and who the shuckers and jivers were—the teachers who were only going through the motions, putting on a show, and collecting a paycheck. In most schools, I've found, about 10 percent of teachers are stars; another 10 percent are shuckers and jivers. The vast majority are well-meaning strugglers; the strugglers can be helped.

I used what I observed in two ways: (1) to develop my schedule for further classroom observations, focusing on shuckers and jivers first, well-meaning strugglers next, and stars last; and (2) to establish what our in-house staff development program would include.

To explain the second point first: If I observed that a lot of staff needed help with a specific teaching skill, like asking thought-provoking questions, we'd have staff development sessions on good question-

ing techniques during our regular faculty and departmental conferences, and spend only five to ten minutes on "administrivia." Such a talk
might be led by me or by one of the star teachers who was particularly
skilled in the area being discussed. In this way, every faculty meeting
and department meeting became an opportunity for teachers to grow
professionally.

Further classroom visits began in October. These were 45-minute,
full-period classroom observations—starting with the poorest faculty,
because they were the chief destroyers of kids' chances for success. During the observation, I wrote down everything that was on the board,
noted how many kids were in attendance, how many and which kids
recited, what was on the walls, and—most important—*whether there
was evidence that the kids were learning anything.*

Mr. Littwin once said to me, "Lorraine, if the kids don't know any
more at the end of the period than they knew at the beginning, the lesson is unsatisfactory." Obvious, isn't it? But how hard this was to tell
some earnest people who would say, in all sincerity, "I taught it, I covered the curriculum, but they didn't learn it." Or, "I taught that lesson,
Ms. Monroe, but ninety percent of them failed my test that Friday."

"You taught it, but they didn't learn it is oxymoronic." Often I had to
say this three times before the significance of the statement *they didn't
learn it!* got through to them. It was almost always what I call the earnest
strugglers—the hard-working, well-meaning, but untrained and
unskilled teachers—who got it. Once they did, we could go on to have
collegial conversations about methods and techniques to help kids
learn what they were taught.

The first few strugglers who came into my office for a postobservation conference were slightly fearful. They were thinking, "Sure, she said
she wanted to be 'collegial,' but after all she is the principal, she rates my
job performance, and *she sat in the back of the room writing the whole
goddamned time!*" So I would break the ice by always offering tea or coffee and then start by gently giving my overall assessment of the lesson
that I had observed.

"This was a pretty good lesson," I might begin, and the person would relax and take a deep breath. Then I'd say, "Did you realize you only called on six kids out of the twenty-eight in the class?"

"No, did I?" was the usual answer.

"Did you realize you asked multiple questions, like 'So who were the carpetbaggers? Why were they called carpetbaggers? What part did they play during the post–Civil War era?' Which question did you want the kids to answer?"

"No, did I?"

We'd then begin the give-and-take of exploring how to consciously spread out student recitation, maybe by trying to call on children in a variety of patterns (boxes, circles, Xs, Zs) until inclusion becomes a habit. As we talked and I shared my own experiences and war stories from my first teaching assignment, the strugglers laughed in relief, knowing that they were not incompetent, just untaught in the ways of controlling kids, material, and time—the three nemeses of new teachers. Telling them about my own teaching days helped forge a bond between us and established my credibility as a coach and mentor.

Ultimately, the postobservation conference ended with the teacher feeling buoyed up. And gradually the news spread that I was true to my word about my purpose in observing—not to attack teachers but to help them. I loved these collegial conversational training sessions. In importance and love, they paralleled my informal talks with kids. I get a rush now thinking of how much I enjoyed these two aspects of my work as a leader.

Addition by Subtraction

However, this message meant nothing to the truly recalcitrant incompetent ("I've been teaching this way for years and was never marked Unsatisfactory before") or the irremediable incompetent ("I've tried everything you suggested, but nothing works. These kids can't do, won't do, don't do, couldn't care less. They're not like us when you and I went to school—they're not even like the kids who used to be here when the school first opened").

One of the pitifully incompetent ones—I'll call him Mr. Grindley—told me, "You should have seen me years ago when the *other* kids were here. I could really teach then." (Back in the 1940s and '50s, the students at Taft had been predominantly white. Now they were 48 percent African-American, 48 percent Latino, and 2 percent Asian—with one white boy.) My response was, "The other kids are not coming back, so you're going to have to really teach *these* kids."

He never did; he really couldn't. Mr. Grindley wasn't evil; he was just misplaced and miserably unhappy. No one had told him years ago that he should try another profession. He felt stuck—too old, he thought, to get into any other profession, but just a few years too young to retire with a livable pension, so he stayed.

I gave Mr. Grindley a rating of U—rating Unsatisfactory—at the end of the year. The chapter chair for the United Federation of Teachers, the union, came to me and said, "Ms. Monroe, I've come to ask you to rescind Grindley's U rating. If you do, he promises to transfer." (In New York City, a teacher with five years of experience can apply for a transfer to another school with a faculty vacancy.) "What do you say?"

"Hoffman," I said, "I gave Grindley the U he deserved. Tell him he should transfer anyway."

Grindley did transfer to another high school. His new principal called me the first day and said, "Lorraine, what do I got here?"

"Just what you see," I said. "Good luck."

A few incompetent teachers were harder to get rid of. Some remedial math and reading teachers at Taft liked to have children do individual work in folders during class time. Like lots of methods, individual work done in moderation is fine. However, when it's done 45 minutes each day for forty weeks a year, it's counterproductive, particularly if the teacher doesn't check the folder work each day and doesn't walk around the room to assist students with individual problems but rather sits at the desk and sees just three to five students each period.

This was the M.O. of one remedial math teacher. After observing this ineffective behavior for a brief time, I instituted a policy that required teaching the whole class a skill in the beginning of the period. After that, students could practice the skill and attend to individual work in their folders. This man resisted this policy change and adhered to his accustomed "drill and kill" methods; so I began to observe him frequently.

One day when he came into the room, I was already seated in the back. When he saw me, he quickly filled the blackboard with twenty-five simple math examples. Going over these took most of the period; then it was back to folder work.

In our postobservation conference, when I asked where the twenty-five math examples came from, since I never saw him refer to a plan, he pointed to his temple and replied, "Why, where all numbers come from—the mind of man." He'd had no plan for the class, and his made-up examples were irrelevant to what he'd been teaching and to what he should have been teaching. I knew then that he was moving rapidly toward an Unsatisfactory rating for the year. He knew it, too.

Like all staffs, the staff at Taft High School knew who the incompetents were. In every organization, staff members talk about who is on the ball and who isn't; they all wonder whether the leader knows, and what she will do about it. In this case, they also knew something I did not: that this teacher was a "proney" (someone prone to accidents). They even laid bets as to when his "accident" would happen each year. As I was told later, January or February were the usual months. This took him out of school—with pay—for the spring term.

So when he was hit in the back of the head by "an unknown black assailant wearing a navy blue windbreaker" in late January (so said his accident report), no one was surprised except me.

He returned the next year, still unreformed and again earning an Unsatisfactory rating. The last accident occurred in his classroom; he caught his foot on a loose board near the radiator and fell down, striking his head so hard that he lay unmoving and semiconscious until several colleagues came to rescue him. Out again—with pay.

Over time, he compiled a record of twelve accidents before he was out of the school system.

It was my practice when observing to try to be in the classroom at the beginning of the period so that I could observe everything from the minute the class began to the very end; first, because I loved observing the entire drama, and second, because I knew that if I came in late to a poor teacher's room he or she would claim, "You should have been there in the beginning—you missed the best part." Conversely, if I left before the end of the period, he or she would say, "You should have stayed— the lesson crescendoed and was splendid at the end."

Often staying a full 45 minutes in a poor teacher's classroom gave me an instant migraine. I always thought, "How good these kids are! This teacher is so awful the kids should all be throwing things at him or rushing up to choke him."

Anyway, one day early in my tenure at Taft, I wanted to observe a relatively new math teacher. I came before he arrived and sat in the middle seat of the last row directly facing his desk. The kids filed in, greeted me, and sat down. Four minutes into the period, he came shambling through the back door into the room past me and up the side aisle to his desk. He threw his briefcase on the desk and said, "Okay, do the busy-work on the board."

He sat down and began to call the roll. All the while, various kids turned around and winked and grinned at me. Finally, he saw me. "Okay, so who are you? The new girl in the class?"

"No," I replied, "I'm the principal."

"Oh, shit!" he said as he shot up out of his chair.

The kids cracked up laughing. "All right!" he announced. "As we usually do, class, copy the homework for tonight and get started on the Do-Now that I'm going to put on the board!"

A boy turned to me and said, "Usually we don't do hardly anything. You should come every day!" I told his chairman of this visit, and to the teacher's credit, he ultimately became quite a competent math teacher.

Having observed everybody in September, I began to zero in on the two most incompetent staff members during October. Soon thereafter, as I was walking down the first-floor hallway, someone came up quickly behind my right ear and without breaking stride said, "How did you get to be so smart so soon?" I knew that the person was referring to how I had spotted and begun to zero in on the chief incompetents.

My doing so was therapeutic. Most of the staff, I found, really wanted to teach. They'd been waiting for someone to come along to remind them of their mission, someone who knew excellence and supported it. They were pleased that I could recognize and distinguish between the untutored incompetent who would profit from assistance and the downright "Fuck this work" incompetent for whom assistance meant nothing.

I got "so smart so soon" because I looked, and because I knew what I was looking at and what I was looking for. It's one of the simple keys to being an effective leader.

It's harder to eliminate incompetent or uncaring staff in education than in business. Thanks to civil service laws and union contracts, teachers have administrative and legal recourse when their abilities are challenged, and elaborate procedures are in place to protect their rights. I'm all for due process, but in the New York City school system the rules are used all too often to keep ineffective teachers on the job.

When a principal wants to dismiss an incompetent teacher, she must start with a file of letters and memos documenting the teacher's ineffectiveness and showing that coaching and assistance have been provided over time, to no avail. In virtually every case, the teacher will file an appeal, which must be adjudicated through up to three levels of hearings, at each of which the principal must appear to prove her case. I've seen this procedure followed even when teachers were guilty of blatantly uncaring behavior—for example, by being late to school fifty times in a single year. The usual outcome is that the teacher's Unsatisfactory rating by the principal remains on his record, and he remains in the same school or elsewhere in the system.

Rising Above Pettiness

The well-meaning strugglers are another matter altogether. They need and deserve the best help we can provide. There are compelling, quantifiable reasons for paying attention to teachers who need help in the classroom. Take a well-meaning struggler with an average class load. If, for example, he or she has a program of five classes a day with 30 kids per class, that adds up to 150 kids a semester who are poorly taught and therefore damaged. If he or she has a switch in classes at midyear, that's 300 kids ill-used per year. And if he or she remains in the school system for twenty-five years, that's either 3,750 kids or 7,500 kids damaged.

It was distasteful for me to go after the recalcitrant incompetents. I hate doing it because it forces me to spend a lot of time in the company of a teacher I would otherwise avoid like the plague. Later, I have to defend my professional judgment across the grievance table where the UFT defends the teacher's behavior by accusing me of being arbitrary and capricious. More especially, I resent the documenting and defending necessary, because it takes time away from helping staff who are remediable, time away from supporting my stars, and time away from spinning out innovative programs, one of my chief sources of pleasure. I hope that no one, UFT or the incompetents, thought I got my jollies from cracking down on bad teachers. It's just something a principal has to do. School is about the kids.

After the Grindley incident, I realized that the UFT chapter chair at Taft was anti-administration in ways that made no sense. The school was more orderly than it had been in years, and staff morale was high by all indications: people were laughing and smiling, volunteering more, and filing fewer official complaints (grievances). Yet the UFT chapter hacks tried to encourage grievances. They grieved—and lost grievances—over demands for compensatory time (out of classroom) for which staff were not qualified, and over complaints about oversized classes that were reduced whenever possible. The UFT chapter chair was even overheard hawking grievances in the hall outside my office: "Any grievances? Anybody got any grievances?"

Several staff members came to me to say, "Don't take it personally, Ms. Monroe. It's the same old three or four disgruntled ones who used to plague Ms. Pulitzer before you. They're better than they used to be. Actually, they have nothing to grieve about."

Intellectually I understood this, and professionally I withstood them, but emotionally I found the UFT position in my school profoundly exasperating. Did they like the old way—with its chaos, unpredictability, and laissez-faire supervision—better? I guess some very few did. For others, the confrontational style they had developed over the years, which may have been justified in times when the school administrators were incompetent or uncaring, had simply become a habit.

It feels odd to me to speak critically of the teachers' union. As a new teacher, I had gone on strike—willingly, though reluctantly—in defense of the UFT's right to exist. My parents had both been union members, and I certainly knew that the conditions in which they worked—especially when my mother worked in a garment-industry sweatshop—needed improving. Of course, teachers are not "laborers" in the sense my parents were. But I could see that, for example, the overloaded schedule I was given when I started teaching was unfair and should have been rectified. A union that would fight on behalf of teachers was important.

In the years since then, however, I've felt that for many union leaders, working conditions have taken precedence over helping children—which is, after all, the reason we become teachers. And the protection of documented incompetents among school faculties is unconscionable. I hope that today's teachers' unions are getting back to their original values and refocusing attention where it belongs—on the children.

During my tenure at Taft, the assistant principals—Peter Engel and Cal Martin—and I met monthly with the leaders of the UFT chapter to hear their "concerns." Almost from Day One, they were trivial and later predictable: "Out-of-classroom jobs equitably distributed," "Requirements on posting time jobs," "Extra time for marking exams," and "Oversized classes." There was one last UFT complaint bastion, as Mr. Littwin had warned me. When all else is going smoothly, the union is sure to complain about the nebulous "Low staff morale."

We always took careful notes during their litany of grumbles and took care of what we could quickly, answering them in writing. The meetings became a ritualistic dance: we'd all sit, they would complain, we would take notes, we would fix what we could and respond to the chapter chair in writing.

For our first union chapter meeting, I put out coffee, tea, and cookies. They didn't touch a thing: Eat the enemies' food? Not us, no way. So Cal, Peter, and I ate it when they left. One time, however, I put out pâté, cheeses, breads, and crackers from Zabar's, the fancy New York gourmet shop (they were left over from an earlier meeting). This time, they ate the enemies' food, and it got back to me that they bragged to their colleagues from other schools, "Does *your* principal feed you Zabar's?"

I rose above their pettiness by watching the school and teachers change under my leadership. A real clincher for me was the day I came back to my office and found a rose and a note on my desk: "Thank you for giving us back our school." It was signed by a student.

"We'll Make Them Honors!"

We'd made progress in some basic ways: restoring order to the school, eliminating some of the incompetent teachers, and encouraging and helping those who wanted to teach well. But it wasn't enough. I realized that Taft was not attracting the neighborhood's best and brightest because of its reputation of being "a bad school." Many students were using tricks to enroll at other schools—for example, giving the address of a relative in another district as their own address. I realized that we had to prove to the community and the kids themselves that academic excellence at Taft was not just a matter of history, and that our students were capable of achieving great things.

When I announced to the staff that I wanted to start an honor school at Taft, one teacher came to me and said, "You can't have an honor school here."

"Why not?" I asked.

"Because there are no more white kids here."

"Look at my face and tell me that again," I said. He backed away.

I asked a counselor to form an honor-school class of twenty-five kids from among our pool of incoming ninth-graders. She did her best to select likely candidates, but when she gave me their record cards she warned me, "Here they are—the best that was sent to us—but in no other place would they be considered honor students."

"That's okay," I said as I took them. "We'll make them honors."

I sat with my assistants and we decided which teachers in each department were the best. The honors class would have these teachers for their major subjects. I also decided that they would have these same teachers for two years in a row, to establish continuity and encourage bonding. For the same reason, I gave them Sheila Orner as their counselor for their entire four years at Taft.

The program worked. For lots of reasons—among them good teaching, good counseling, special prep classes for the PSAT college entrance exam, and other special attention—they thrived and became honor students by any set of standards. All were accepted to college; one went into the Marines first, and we even cracked the Ivies and the former "seven sisters": Brown, Columbia, Smith, and Mount Holyoke.

We made it a regular practice to cultivate "average" students who were thought by their teachers to have potential by placing them in pre-honor-school programs. I examined where we were succeeding and where we were failing, and I discovered that if we kept kids past the ninth grade we pretty much had them hooked to an uninterrupted march to graduation, barring any cataclysmic life circumstances (such as addiction or pregnancy). So we began to break the ninth grade up into small clusters/groups/houses of 150 students. We assigned these clusters some of the same teachers for two years and added a family assistant to each, whose job was to mail notes and to call home when students were absent or chronically late.

We also wanted to create a for-credit community-service program for our kids. Getting the funding proved to be an interesting challenge. We needed a $14,000 increase in our budget—what the school bureaucracy calls "a 0.5 percent allotment increase"—to make this program possible. We submitted the appropriate request several times, but each time the district superintendent refused. Finally, I called on the superintendent myself. When all of my arguments failed, I played my last card: "You know," I told him, "I don't need this job. They're looking for smart black women at the telephone company."

I'd simply made that up, but the ploy worked. The superintendent stared at me for a long moment, then picked up his phone and ordered the budget increase.

The program turned out to be quite successful. We scheduled our kids' core courses in the morning and sent them off to various community sites in the afternoon. Again, the special attention paid off; the kids loved the community service in the politician's office, the local day-care centers, and a senior citizens' residence on the Grand Concourse.

The latter proved to be the best service placement. Ironically, it was because the older folks whom the kids helped were so grouchy! They were less than pleased when our kids arrived late to take them out to the bank or shopping, and they let the kids know it in no uncertain terms. "Where were you? You're fifteen minutes late! Now we'll have a long wait in the bank line, all because of your laziness. I thought you were a responsible boy." At our biweekly debriefing meetings, the kids told us that they so disliked the old peoples' nagging about lateness that they made it their business to be on time.

We heard some insightful comments from our students when we asked what they were learning from these experiences. One boy said, "You know, it was funny; when we first came, those old ladies would grab their purses and hold them tight and close to them."

"Really," I said. "What was your reaction? How did you feel?"

"We didn't pay them no mind. I guess at first they thought we were gonna rob them or something, but after a while they relaxed. It's kind of hard to dance clutchin' your pocketbook."

"You dance with them?" I asked, somewhat incredulous.

"Yeah, the old ladies love to dance."

Another student was silent for a while, then volunteered, "You know what I learned? I thought that when people got old, they got wise, but I learned they don't."

"What makes you say that?" I asked.

"Well, I see how they sit in the lounges all segregated: the whites sit together, the blacks sit together. I'm disappointed, because I thought by the time people got old, race wouldn't matter." I had no answer for him, but I thought, "What incredible experiences and lessons these kids are getting!"

A Core of Believers

No leader can single-handedly make an institution better. The leader can inspire, articulate the dream, monitor and evaluate and tinker with the series of actions that makes the dream happen, but the people actually live the dream and make it real. At Taft, I had the good fortune to be surrounded from the beginning by a small core of believers. They were my assistant principals, a few teachers in every department, support staff, and great custodians. They all caught my vision and my seriousness. Improvement at Taft was a long-term dream plan, acted out day to day by ordinary and extraordinary people.

One of the extraordinary people was my assistant principal in charge of guidance, pupil personnel services, and anything else I requested of him, Peter H. Engel. He was at Taft a year before I came, and arrived in a strange, perhaps fateful way—he found his letter of appointment to Taft mysteriously covered by leaves on his lawn.

Our styles were quite different: mine noisy, using broad strokes, seemingly frenetic but ultimately focused on results; his was methodical and orderly, the style of a control fanatic systematically getting things done. Yet, strangely, after some time we found that we could read each other's thoughts and would come to work concerned about the same issues and with a plan for addressing them. After a while, we almost didn't have to speak in whole sentences. No wonder that when I was asked to serve at the Central School Board at 110 Livingston Street, I chose him for my assistant.

I inherited another good person, Karen Grayson, who was our community liaison. I don't know what that title meant in the past, but I know how we configured the position. Karen got to know the members of the 172nd Street Merchants Association and most of the other movers and shakers in the community. Through her work, we got job and intern placements for our older kids, speakers for our assemblies (like Herman Badillo, who was Bronx borough president then), exhibition space in banks and stores, and donations of food for our kids who participated in walkathons.

Karen also organized the annual Friends of Taft luncheon. To this luncheon—proudly catered by our Home Economics Department—we invited everyone in the community who had helped us: politicians, investors, businessmen, parents' association officers, and heads of community agencies and institutions like Bronx Lebanon Hospital. This was our chance to thank them, entertain them, feed them, and (not least) discuss our future needs, such as job sites, internships, advocacy, health screenings, and scholarships for needy kids. We almost always received help in all the areas mentioned.

I think public relations is an important aspect of any principal's job. I worked hard at it. I addressed school and community boards, visited local middle schools, and made sure that the local district superintendent and community leaders knew and trusted me. Long-term school success requires support from the entire community, and you won't get it unless you ask for it—and earn it.

Simply recognizing and thanking people for their efforts is a leadership tool that is used far too rarely. I hosted a Zabar's breakfast for our secretaries, aides, and paraprofessionals. The secretaries were impressed and pleased at the recognition; they'd never had breakfast with the principal before. But it was the aides and paras—the unappreciated foot soldiers in most schools—who were genuinely moved, not so much by the lox and bagels and different varieties of cheese and pastries as by the fact they had been thought of.

One said as she sat with the others at my conference table, "Gee, we were never in here before. This is the first time I've ever been in the principal's office. It's nice in here."

I responded, "This is to thank you for helping to make it nice out there."

As my time at Taft went on, the good results of our efforts continued to grow. One of the most gratifying was a thousand-dollar grant from a Ford Foundation school-improvement program, which happened this way: I got a letter inviting us to apply for the grant and specifying a list of requirements—describe your school, its demographics, the staff and programs; give evidence as to why and how you've improved, the effects of the improvement, and to what you attribute the improvement and if you're chosen how you will spend the $1,000. It concluded, "Send in the accompanying postcard indicating whether or not you intend to apply."

I tore up the postcard and threw it away. I figured I would spend at least $5,000 worth of staff and administration time filling out the application. And what would I get? I thought the most likely outcome would be a check for $1,000 of what we call "categorical money"—that is, money that can only be used to buy things in a specified category. Who needs it?

I got an identical postcard a week later and wrote across it, "Don't care to apply" and mailed it off.

A week later, I got a call from Superintendent Folchi. "Lorraine," he said, "did you get the Ford Foundation postcard?"

"Yes, but . . ." and I went on to explain my rationale for not applying. He said, "Apply anyway," and so we did.

As I predicted, it took a lot of hours to fill out the proposal forms. In doing so, however, my assistant principals came up with two findings. One, that we had done a lot of great stuff. They were surprised that we'd done so much, because we'd never sat down and consciously catalogued all the programs and all their effects on our kids. Two, when asked to identify the single factor most responsible for the positive changes, they came up with the answer, the principal. Thankfully, I was not there when they came to that conclusion; I would have been pleased but embarrassed.

The Ford Foundation grant was one important outside validation of the work we'd done at Taft. Another came toward the end of the first year, when two senior principals came to check on what I had done. I knew from my experience of such inspections at Stevenson that I needed to save every memo, every bulletin, every letter, every edict . . . every piece of evidence concerning what I had administered, supervised, and caused to happen. Engel and Martin dressed up for the occasion. I was concerned, but I wasn't nervous—I knew we had done good work.

I offered to take the principals on a tour of the school, but one savvy principal peeled off and said, "I want to go around alone." (He knew that school tours are usually planned and designed to skirt all the "problem" areas.) When we saw him later, he said, "I checked the back stairs— you can tell a lot about a school from the back stairs."

The principals asked about what we'd done in each major category of school activity—guidance, discipline/security, staff development, student achievement, attendance, union, parents—and we showed him the written evidence. One then asked, "Tell me, Lorraine. How did you manage to do so much in one year when you were only an interim acting principal, two whole steps from being tenured?"

I said, "I've never been 'interim acting' anything. I couldn't do this job believing that I was 'interim acting' anything. I believed Dr. Macchiarola when he told me to go be principal. That's exactly what I did."

He smiled and said, "You've done quite a job here."

A Time to Celebrate

Sometime after Thanksgiving, I looked around and saw that parts of the dream were happening. I thought we should have a staff Christmas party to celebrate our hard work. I let the word go out that I needed to see the "party animals." Very soon, two guys from the gym department and the chief security officer came to my door and said in chorus, "We heard you're looking for the party animals."

One said, "Are you serious about having a party?"

"Yes—why?"

"The other principal didn't like parties and would not let us have one," he replied, sounding like a complaining teenager.

"Can you guys set it up?"

"Yeah—sure. You want it here on school property?"

"Yes," I said. "The June party we'll have off the grounds at a nice place."

"The June party!" they echoed, nearly out of their minds with glee— *two* parties! December and June! "Any liquor allowed?"

"Just punch."

"Okay, punch," they said, and off they went.

December came. The kids were dismissed, and I was in my office with Cal Martin and Peter Engel. We were tired and pretty despondent over the financial allotment we'd just received for the spring term. It wasn't good, especially because I was paying back the former principal's overestimation of enrollment. (I was too naive then to balk at paying for a previous colleague's errors.) But on December 23, there wasn't any point in protesting. It was time to party.

When we got to the student cafeteria in the basement, the entire staff was there, seated quietly. "These are party animals?" I thought. Since I go to parties to dance, I said to the hired DJ, "Crank up the volume," and went over and asked Frank Mauriello to dance.

Well, that did it. There was a rush to the floor, and even people who couldn't dance got up and made all kinds of ancient tribal movements from every ethnicity imaginable. One teacher, a Mr. Flaherty, got up and wound himself into some kind of Celtic jig that he never stopped, assisted, I think, by the punch and by the whole group's reckless and wild release.

It was right to shake loose after working so very fiercely and successfully for four solid months. People ate and laughed and danced. It was great to see my staff enjoying a few hours of well-deserved abandon. When I left, late in the evening, Mr. Flaherty was still jigging and circling with his eyes closed and arms raised, a living symbol of our first triumphant semester.

On Pursuing Excellence

You can't *ease* your way to excellence. "You have to burn from the first bar." (Sting)

~

Don't believe that more people, wealth, or things will make a community great. Greatness grows from people with dedication.

~

Some people are born magicians, able to do wonders in their work. But everyone can learn to make a contribution. Excellence takes both kinds.

~

A cadre of creatively crazy, concerned individuals can carry an organization. But *pockets* of excellence don't create the hum an excellent organization has.

~

When you compete, don't just hope to win. *Plan* to *blow away* the competition.

CHAPTER 8

How to Find and Feed the "Creatively Crazy"

INSPIRING INNOVATION

The continued existence and vitality of any organization depends on the leader's ability to evoke, support, and reward innovation. In my experience, organizations can die in two ways:

1. when they move away from the core principles of their mission providing excellence and stability (order)

2. when they fail to creatively come up with new ways to make their mission happen—in other words, to innovate

Innovation in this sense is what my years at Taft were all about. I hope I haven't made the changes at Taft High School sound simple and easy. In one way, they were, because most members of our team really did enjoy dreaming up new programs and projects to benefit the kids, and they were delighted to have their creative energies liberated at last.

But on a day-to-day basis, there's no denying that the work was hard. Teaching is never easy, and I was challenging our teachers in ways in which they'd rarely been challenged before. Those who'd formerly hidden behind the chaos in the school and used it as an excuse for not producing had had their major justification taken away. But we tried to provide those who really wanted to teach with an environment and a program conducive to learning and to creating exciting new programs for making educational magic. And we pursued this goal—a quiet, orderly, effective school—through a series of simple steps.

Simple Acts That Set the Stage for Innovation

1. Floor patrols and strictly enforced rules prohibiting students from leaving the classroom during the first 15 minutes or the last 10 minutes of a class period. This worked wonders in reducing noise and disorder and allowing students and teachers to focus on learning.

2. Establishing other non-negotiable rules and regulations, and making sure that there were real consequences when the rules were broken.

3. Creating an expectation of intense, bell-to-bell teaching with constant monitoring for teacher improvement and student learning.

4. Developing a rigorous academic program that proved to our kids that they could meet high intellectual expectations with proper teaching and support.

5. Offering an extensive preschool and postschool extracurricular-activity program that appealed to all kids, from nerds to jocks. This helped keep our students off the streets and gave them additional

opportunities to bond with teachers while focusing on productive, creative activities.

All of this was done with the support and efforts of the majority of our staff, who were willing to put in the work and the time to make real change happen for the benefit of our kids. Two individuals—Karen Grayson, our community liaison, and Roberta Goldman, the coordinator of student activities—were especially important in making this crucial program work.

With basic order restored, we were ready to begin the magical part of our mission: making Taft an exciting place to learn.

How Change Begins

When I share my ideas with other leaders who are struggling to improve their own organizations, I am often asked, "Well, Dr. Monroe, suppose I don't have such a dedicated staff. How can I make positive changes happen?" I think the answer involves several important points.

First, if you are working in a dispirited or ineffective organization, realize that *you* as leader will have to be the first staff person to believe that quality and excellence are possible with the staff you have. I was that person. Change must begin with you.

Once you've formulated your ideas for making positive changes happen, to begin implementing those ideas realize that you don't need to have 100 percent of your staff believing in them. At Taft, I led a total staff of over two hundred people, but in the early days, the believers and innovators numbered around thirty persons. That included my eleven assistant principals, my secretary, and the school custodians—the creative, risk-taking core who bought into the program early. I supported, congratulated, stroked, and fed these people, and they produced the early results that gradually convinced others to join us.

Next, the leader of change must take every opportunity to communicate and reinforce the new ideas he or she is trying to teach. Use meetings, memos, letters, and constant one-on-one conversations to hammer home the need for change and the benefits it can bring.

But always make your appeal on the basis of your organization's mission and the worthiness of the work you share. Most people, I believe, have a core of idealism in their hearts—a sense of passion and purpose that originally led them to choose their life's work. Certainly this is true in education. Teacher salaries are still woefully inadequate, especially in comparison to the impact and consequences teachers' work has on society as a whole. So no one goes into teaching for the money. I found it important to remind my staff constantly about why they chose to be teachers. I'm sure that a similar appeal can be effective in many other professional fields where the work, at its core, makes a contribution to the betterment of the world.

In my experience, a surprising number of staff will come forward to do extra work and offer extra creativity on behalf of the organization and its mission—and at a place like Taft, that mission was changing the lives of the kids we served. Staff will *not* respond if the effort seems designed to benefit you. Examine your own motives! If you as leader are doing the work to promote yourself—your career, your reputation, or your chance to move up in some hierarchy—any hint of this will kill staff initiative. The appeal must always be "It's about our mission. It's about kids." And that commitment must be genuine, not a pretense.

I've taught, managed, spoken, and consulted in schools all over the United States and in several foreign countries. I've never found a school, no matter how shabby it may seem at first glance, that was completely devoid of staff members who were talented, energetic, and ready and willing to do "creatively crazy," positive things for kids. But staff members in any organization will not step forward to offer that extra effort unless their leader explicitly asks for innovation and well-thought-out risk taking, supports those who have great ideas, and who herself personally models the behavior requested.

This creatively crazy, innovative work can be politically risky; every organization has its political hacks, time servers, and incompetents who resent change and want to withhold their energy and commitment. But the alternatives to risk taking are deadly. Doing nothing, running scared, and second-guessing kills initiative, blights creativity, and ultimately sabotages the organization and the good work it should be accomplishing.

Asking for Innovation

Shortly after I arrived at Taft, I sent out an explicit call for innovation in one Friday's staff bulletin:

If you have an idea that's about kids and encouraging their achievement that you'd like to have support for—see me.

A couple of days later, Mr. Millstein, a quiet, slightly built, red-haired economics and civics teacher in our Social Studies Department, came to see me.

"I have an idea," he said diffidently. "I'm trying to get my students to understand how city government agencies work. I thought that if we put a consumer education booth in the local bank, my students could run the booth. We could invite people who are having difficulty with a city agency or a utility company to leave their questions with the students, on a self-addressed postcard for the response. Then, the students could research the answers, write them on the postcards, and mail them out. The kids would learn a lot, and the neighborhood people would benefit."

I said, "Sounds great to me, but you need to ask the bank president."

Mr. Millstein was one step ahead of me. He said, "I already have, and he said that if you agree, he agrees."

The program proved to be extremely popular. Hundreds of local people got help with their questions and problems, and the students got all kinds of real-world learning they could never have gotten any other way. Our kids also enjoyed their fifteen minutes of fame as a result of this program. The kids and the bank manager were on the evening news of a major TV network together, and a photo appeared in the newspaper showing the bank manager with one arm around a black kid and another around a Puerto Rican kid. I'm sure it was his first close-up encounter with kids of color.

The manager got to like the kids so much that he invited our students to attend a series of talks about careers in banking in his conference room. Later, he called me and said, "One of your boys is quite intelligent and shows a lot of promise. If you graduate him, our bank will pay his college fees." I thanked him for the offer and hung up the phone and wrote a memo to his counselor: "Whatever it takes, find a way to *graduate this boy!*" We did, and the bank kept its promise.

Mr. Millstein's creativity didn't stop there. Later, he proposed putting a similar booth in the local hospital. I said, "If the hospital administrator says yes . . ." He interrupted, "I already asked, and he said if you say yes, then he says yes." This program was just as successful as the first.

Soon he approached me again with a different idea. "How about having my students tutor the fifth- and sixth-graders in the local elementary school in reading? They can use the *Junior Consumer Reports* as reading material." I repeated my by-now-familiar line: "If the elementary school principal says yes, then I say yes." And he replied as usual, "I already asked her, and she said if you say yes, then she'll say yes."

Other teachers began coming in with ideas. A biology teacher asked, "Can I take a class out on a barge to dredge the Hudson River to study local water pollution?" Why not? She said, "It will cost five dollars per kid. I've checked, and I know that we can fund the trip from Student Council funds, but I think we should ask the kids to contribute one dollar each." She was off and running.

Another faculty member, English teacher Barbara Armellino, proved to be a treasure. She volunteered to start and run a chapter of Arista, the national student honor society. Next thing I knew, she was asking, "How about a Junior Arista?" And once Junior Arista was in place, Barbara was at my elbow again, asking, "Can't we reopen the Student Store we used to have at Taft?"

For once, I was doubtful. "But Barbara," I asked, "who would run it? You can't do it—you're already organizing two Arista groups, running the Needlepoint 745 Club, and teaching your English classes. Isn't that enough?"

"I know I can't do it, but my mom can. She's a retired accountant and bookkeeper, and she's sitting around the house going stir-crazy. She'd be glad to volunteer. My brother will come in to help paint the store and set up the shelves, and my father will put new locks on the door."

So the Armellinos did all of that, and soon the store was a profitable source of school funds for financing still other innovative programs and helping with student emergencies—clothing, eyeglasses, emergency carfare, or application fees for special programs.

The 745 Clubs

A moment ago, I mentioned Barbara's Needlepoint 745 Club. Let me explain how that came about. Each morning when I arrived at my office at Taft, I would look out my window and notice a lot of kids hanging out in front of the school, some as early as 7:15. One morning, it dawned on me that there was a group of teachers who also arrived early. I got an idea. In next Friday's staff bulletin, this note appeared:

> If you're an early bird who comes to school before 7:45 in the morning, and you'd like to volunteer to share your hobby or special skill with students who also come early, please put a note in my box.

About twenty teachers responded. Thus began a fine program, which we named the 745 clubs. Each club had its special interest. They included poetry, gardening, needlepoint, chess, biking, body building, cooking, sewing, and track. The sewing and cooking clubs became junior enterprises when the girls began marketing and selling their creations. For instance, the members of the cooking club (who happened to be a group of special education students) baked and sold nut breads, taking orders from students and teachers on Monday for delivery later in the week.

As with all of our special programs, we made sure that the clubs served more than one purpose. Before the clubs started, I met with the volunteer faculty advisors and asked them to keep their ears open during the club meetings, in case kids might say something that would give us a clue or insight into how we could help them. You see, kids will often open their hearts and speak about their special problem or pain while in the midst of doing things with their hands. For many kids, that's easier than opening up to a counselor in an office. More often, while mixing a batter or working on an engine, kids will reveal astounding fears or beliefs, or "a problem that this friend of mine is having." So our teachers were cautioned to be sensitive and alert, and to notify the counselors if anything important came up.

Soon after the 745 clubs were launched, the chapter chair of the UFT, the teachers' union, paid me a visit. "I see you've got teachers coming in at 7:45 in the morning, earlier than their required time. Don't you know that you can't make teachers work longer than their six-hour, twenty-minute contractual time?"

"That's true," I responded, "but I haven't required anyone to come in early. They volunteered to help the children. I don't believe the union contract says anything about volunteering, does it?"

I had him there. He shook his head and left, and the 745 clubs went on doing their good work for our kids.

More Innovations

Some of our innovations were directly tied to academic achievement. When I arrived at Taft, one of my early questions was, "How do the students in the junior class perform when they take the PSAT?"

The Preliminary Scholastic Achievement Test is a kind of "preview" of the longer, full-fledged SAT exam that students take when applying to colleges. It is also used as a qualifying test for certain scholarships. In most high schools, all college-bound students take the PSAT as a matter of course. But when I asked about PSAT scores at Taft, I was told, "Oh, our kids don't take it."

All that changed during my time at Taft. Not only did we make sure that our juniors took the exam, we also made sure that they were properly prepared for it by a mandatory PSAT study course. It was taught by the chair of our Math Department, Frank Mauriello, and it was largely responsible for some impressive test scores received by our students.

Then there were innovations that simply added to the quality of life for all of us at Taft. When Sy Duchan took me on my first tour of Taft a few days before I took over as principal, I noticed something: a terrace outside the second floor of the building. "Hmm," I thought. "A patio, a porch—some real, live outdoor space. This has possibilities."

Eventually, we put that space to good use. Inspired by the annual spring art shows in Greenwich Village that I'd visited with my students in the past, we instituted our own spring art shows at Taft, using our terrace as an outdoor exhibit space. In later years, these became pretty elaborate: a string quartet made up of four of our talented students played classical music while their classmates toured the exhibit, and punch and cookies were served as a final genteel touch.

We also used art as a way of reaching out to the neighborhood, holding art exhibits in a nearby park to proudly share our kids' work with the community.

A Leader Takes Risks

Making changes means making waves, and it's inevitable that some people become nervous when change happens. It's particularly true in bureaucratic, tradition-bound organizations like our public schools. I've found that a leader can't wait around for a consensus of opinion to support her before she begins innovating. If you do that, nothing will ever happen. Sometimes, you simply have to act first and seek support later. If you know what you are doing and it is the right thing for the mission, then everything will work out in the end.

I developed the habit of never asking my superiors at the Board of Education for permission to carry out any innovation or other "risky" venture. I felt that if I asked, they would usually say no. After all, they were cautious, conservative people, interested in keeping their present jobs or moving up within the hierarchy. Taking risks isn't a good way of accomplishing either goal.

Instead of asking for permission, I would take counsel with myself, reflecting with pen and paper on the pros and cons of the new idea I was considering and trying to measure it against the mission of the school—to help kids. If the positives outweighed the negatives, and if the idea held promise of supporting our mission in a powerful way, then I'd simply go ahead.

My supervisor would come by the school for periodic visits, and I'd either tell him about our latest venture or let him see it for himself. I figured that it would be hard, even for a dyed-in-the-wool bureaucrat, to try to stop a program that was already running successfully. This approach worked like a charm; the supervisor was generally pleased to realize that the successful new program, whatever it was, had been started under his administration. As the saying goes, "Success has many parents." When something is working, people are always ready and eager to bless it and share the credit.

Sometimes, the chance occurrences of life force a risky choice on the leader. When that happens, there's no substitute for being decisive.

One winter morning, I arrived at Taft in the midst of a major blizzard. It had begun snowing the night before, and the snow continued all through the morning. Travel was difficult, even dangerous, especially for the sizable contingent of our teachers who lived in suburban Rockland County and drove down to the city for work. The braver snow bunnies made it in (and were greeted by plates of doughnuts and pots of coffee), but many of their neighbors and colleagues didn't.

A majority of our students showed up, however. For most of them, school was within walking distance—and it was, after all, where their friends were. Lacking enough teachers to stick to our usual schedule, we scrambled to concoct an emergency plan. We held some regular classes and brought together groups of students for special activities and presentations in the auditorium and the gyms. In this way, we got through periods one, two, and three, and served lunch during periods four and five. Meanwhile, the snow kept falling.

Between periods, I kept calling the office of the district superintendent for instructions. Had any word come down from New York's Central Board of Education about closing the school? We weren't authorized to take such a step on our own. But each time I called, as the snowdrifts kept growing, the reply was always, "No, it's a regular school day."

We'd managed to keep the school under control despite the lack of staff, but as the hours passed, my discomfort grew. Finally, as the lunch hour drew to a close, I decided I had to act. I called in Peter Engel. "Peter," I said, "at the end of period five, we'll dismiss school, using the rapid-dismissal procedure."

"Are you sure?" Peter asked. "It's against the rules to dismiss the students without permission."

"I know, but we just can't hold the kids any longer. There's no real education happening now, and the kids know it. So far, they've behaved splendidly, but how long can we control them like this? Spread the word to the staff and the school guards."

The decision was made. Around 1:30, we dismissed the students without incident. The staff was asked to stay behind for another 45 minutes.

When I returned to my office after the dismissal, my secretary handed me the phone. "Superintendent Folchi is on the line."

"Hi, Lorraine," he said. "How's school?"

"Fine," I said in all honesty—after all, the school *was* fine.

He decided to become a little more specific. "I mean, are there any *students* there?"

"No," I admitted.

"Why not?" he asked.

"Because I felt that to keep them longer, without any meaningful instruction going on, would have given license to a few crazy kids to run around the building, vandalizing and painting graffiti. Closing down was the only safe choice."

Mr. Folchi was dubious. "Well," he replied, "you're going to have to write a letter to Chancellor Macchiarola to explain your behavior."

As I hung up, I wondered how Mr. Folchi had found out about my decision so quickly. I later learned that one of my teachers whose wife was a principal at another school had called her to ask her to dismiss her students as we had done, so that the two of them could get on the highway together before any more snow fell. And she, in turn, had called Superintendent Folchi to say, "May I dismiss my school? Lorraine Monroe has dismissed hers."

As requested, I did write a letter to Frank Macchiarola. I explained my reason for closing the school, adding that when he had sent me to Taft with the injunction, "Go be a principal," I had taken him at his word. It was better for me as the leader to decide to dismiss school rather than face the possibility that the behavior of a few kids could force me to shut down or evacuate the school under duress. Acting as I had meant one thing: the adults were in charge.

Dr. Macchiarola never responded to my letter, but later in the school year I attended a meeting at 110 Livingston Street. As I descended the steps of the building after the meeting, a voice behind me boomed, "Is that Lorraine Monroe, who dismisses school whenever?"

I turned and saw Chancellor Macchiarola, smiling at me. All innocence, I replied, "Why, I don't know what you mean!" As with most of my risk taking, the episode came out all right in the end. Sometimes, the safe but most dangerous choice is to do nothing.

On Making Things New

Remember how crazy you could be as a kid? Hang on to that craziness—it's your source of creativity.

~

Don't expect support from others for your creativity and risk taking. Only *after* your ideas work will support come—and credit be taken!

~

It's sometimes *good* for a creatively crazy maniac to work for an invisible, incompetent, uncaring leader. At least the uncaring leader leaves the maniac room to work her magic.

~

Every day, learn something new, and share it with those around you.

~

Fixing anything—a school, a family, a business, a community—takes time, but people demand changes *immediately*. Better start now!

~

Always be planning to do something new—next week, next month, and next year.

CHAPTER 9

Wars and Alarms

SOME BATTLES YOU WIN . . .

SOME BATTLES YOU LOSE

No course in college or graduate school can adequately prepare you to deal with the human side of leadership. This is especially true in today's public schools, where, sad to say, hostile parents, clueless supervisors, and incompetent complainers are not uncommon. A school leader who is focused on her mission of helping kids is likely to find herself caught off guard by the assaults of these negative people. I'm not speaking here of well-intentioned people who happen to disagree with you, but of people who, for whatever reason, are actively interested in impeding your work and who cannot be appealed to on any rational basis. It takes only a few such people to severely disrupt the life of a school.

If the leader cannot outthink and, when necessary, out-crazy those who try to attack her or her staff, the mission may be imperiled. If the leader backs down or crumbles before an assault, word will quickly spread throughout the school and the community: "You can get what you want if you threaten or act loud and bad." Once that perception takes hold, you're in trouble.

My family background has saved me from such a fate. I am fortunate enough to have had a charming but violent father, a man who brooked no interference and could with a single look silence or empty a room. Over the years, I have learned how to call up the spirit of James Williams when I need it and use that spirit to deal successfully with destructive people.

I feel sorry for any leader who cannot, when necessary, call upon the blood of her most crazy relative and use that inherited insanity to remain fearless and in control when confronted by the most hostile people and situations.

Standing Up for the People Who Stand by You

Loyalty is a two-way street. Sometimes the most important thing a leader can do is to stand up for her people in the face of an unfair attack.

A New York State inspection team came to Taft during our second year. These rituals are an inevitable, sometimes bothersome, but necessary part of school protocol, required as part of the registration review process every school periodically faces. Fortunately, we were well prepared. We knew what the inspectors would be interested in seeing and asking, and we worked hard beforehand to get all our documents, reports, and forms in order. And we were proud of the work we'd done. Taft had changed from a school that kids and parents struggled to avoid into a school they were eager to attend. We knew we deserved a positive evaluation.

The appointed week, the inspection team, led by a Mr. Cartwright, fanned out all over our building, looking at records, inspecting classrooms, talking to staff and department heads, and interviewing students. At the end of their two or three days' stay, the inspection team met with me and my administrative staff to give us the results of their review—a kind of "State of the School" report. The assistant principals and I waited to hear their report with quietly proud anticipation.

Mr. Cartwright began, "Well, Ms. Monroe, things seem to be in *fairly* good order." I bristled at this left-handed compliment. This was not the congratulatory tone I'd expected! And things went downhill from there. He went on, "We noticed that some of your attendance forms were not complete." The special education expert on the inspection team chimed in with a challenge: "Are the appropriate number of students being referred to the resource room?" she asked.

My staff and I began to take notes on the inspectors' comments. Many of them were contradictory. For example, one declared, "There are too many students in bilingual education," only to follow this by asking, "Have all your Spanish-surnamed students been tested for placement in bilingual classes?" On the one hand, "Your out-of-school suspension rates have dropped—discipline seems lax"; on the other hand, "Your non-negotiable rules seem repressive."

The carping continued for about ten minutes—unjustified criticisms mingled with truly picayune comments about trivial paperwork and the like. My team, as you can imagine, was visibly upset. So was I.

Finally, Mr. Cartwright concluded, "Well, that's our oral exit report. We'll be sending you a report in writing. Do you have any comments or questions?"

I stood up, knowing that my response would be closely watched by everyone on my staff. This is what I said:

"Mr. Cartwright, I can't believe what my staff and I have just heard. A year ago, Taft was a school that no kid in the neighborhood wanted to attend. No functionary from the Board of Ed ever visited because of the chaos here. Today, all that has changed, as you well know. Yet all you've given us is inconsequential and inaccurate criticisms. Your remarks are insulting to me and my staff, people who've worked far beyond their contractual obligations to make Taft a safe, quiet, and productive place of learning. We've won a Ford Foundation grant for being one of the most improved schools in the nation. Parents in the community are proud to send their kids here, and parents outside of the community are using phony addresses to get their kids into Taft. Send your report," I concluded, "but I don't accept your criticisms as valid in the face of what we've accomplished." I sat down.

My staff beamed. Mr. Cartwright's staff looked up at him, and he said, "I'm sorry you feel that way, Ms. Monroe, and I'll note your remarks in my report. Thank you for cooperating with my staff." And they left.

My staff stood up and went wild. "You told him! The nerve of them! After all we've done! What were they looking at? Why do they always send people who don't know how to look at schools? When has any of them had to actually deal with live children or staff? That's why they're inspectors, not teachers!"

"Listen," I said. "Let's have some tea and coffee. *I* know we've done well, and *you* know it, too, and that's what counts. Besides, we didn't do it for the inspectors. We did it for the kids."

Years later, after I'd left Taft, Mr. Cartwright spotted me in the street and came over to talk. "Ms. Monroe," he told me, "I want you to know how much I admired the work you and your people did at Taft. The inspection report I wrote was just part of my job." Dumbfounded, I grimaced in response and went on my way.

Thinking Fast

Inspections do have a way of bringing out staff creativity. One instance was the morning of our big first visit from the district superintendent, Mr. Folchi. We knew he was coming, so everyone was on best behavior. The security team and I knew in advance the route of the school tour. The custodians made sure everything was spick-and-span. I wore my best take-the-superintendent-around suit. We had juice, coffee, and pastry for him.

The tour was going well—teachers in every class were on their feet teaching their butts off, kids were seated and engaged—when out of the corner of one eye I saw a kid pop out of a classroom door. *Zip!* Just as quickly, he was snatched back in by his collar before the superintendent could notice. At last, we were on our way back to my office, down to the last few yards of the tour.

"Whew," I thought. "Home free without an incident"—when all of a sudden, ten feet in front of us, two boys began throwing and landing punches on each other. I was aghast. But no kid stopped to watch, no kid egged them on, and almost immediately two security guards appeared out of nowhere. The fight was over more quickly than it had begun, so quickly, in fact, that our little administrative convoy didn't break stride—we just walked around the two kids.

When we got inside my office, I said, "Want some more coffee and pastry, Mr. Folchi?" He turned and looked at me quizzically. "Lorraine, did you see that fight just now?"

"Fight?" I asked. "What fight? Oh, *that* fight! I had it staged so you could see how effective my security is!"

We both laughed, but in his follow-up letter, along with the compliments about the school, Mr. Folchi mentioned the fight. I guess he felt he had to—the school, after all, couldn't be perfect.

Seeing Stars

We balanced our daily diet of academic rigor with periodic good times for the kids with the help of Roberta Goldman, our coordinator of student activities. We held school dances and walkathons and fundraisers and concerts. And occasionally, Roberta was able to lure celebrities to the school as a special treat for our kids. One day, martial artist and movie star Chuck Norris came to the school, and he turned out to be so popular, he had to take refuge in my office. Thank goodness I was out of the building that morning at a meeting.

But I *was* there the day a famous rhythm-and-blues singer came—a lady who'll never receive another invitation from any school of mine. We'd planned a gala reception for her, including an appearance before the students in our auditorium. Things got off to a rocky start, however, when she arrived quite late and unapologetic. She was wearing a full-length mink coat, which she wouldn't condescend to put in my closet but instead gave to one of her bodyguards to hold in the wings off stage.

The auditorium was packed when she finally stepped on stage to greet an audience of excited kids who had sat quietly in anticipation of her gracing our humble place with her presence. Everyone was eager to hear one or two of her famous hit songs. But to my dismay, she did not sing a note. Instead, she delivered the following remarks, each sentence followed by an outburst of heartfelt cheering and applause:

"Hi, gang!" (*Yay!*)

"Thanks for buying my records." (*Yay!*)

"I just came to say school is important, so stay in school so that you can get a good education and be somebody" (*Yay! Yay!*) "in the future." (*Yay!!!*)

"God bless!" (*Yay!*) And she bowed and exited stage left.

My assistants and I, sitting on the stage during this two-minute performance, looked at one another in disgust. Then we looked at our kids' bright shining eyes, so pleased to have been favored with the star's glorious presence. Not one kid grumbled or exclaimed, "What? Not a note, a chorus, nothing?" Just loud applause and "Yays" at her exit.

They had every right to feel cheated and condescended to. But amazingly, there were no hard feelings or disruptions, not even from the thousands outside who could not fit into the auditorium but who'd heard the rumors, "Somebody Big is here!"

After Ms. R&B had been chauffeured away and the kids were dismissed from the auditorium, my assistants and I went to my office, closed the door, thanked God for our wonderfully disciplined kids, and vowed never again to have a Star come to the school without first checking her intentions.

I'm happy to say that this behavior isn't typical of my experience with the wealthy and powerful. Both at Taft and later at the Frederick Douglass Academy, we received much generous support and help from leaders in politics, business, the arts, and the media. At Taft, local businesspeople gave food for our student walkathon on behalf of the March of Dimes, exhibition spaces for our art shows, and other contributions.

At Frederick Douglass, the outpouring of help has been even greater. Gifts of cash and merchandise have made possible our extended program of clubs, tutoring, and activities for kids; an after-school parents' program, including GED preparation classes, English classes, and a women's group; student trips to San Francisco, Montreal, Quebec, England, France, and South Africa; and the purchase of sports equipment, computers for a language lab, and the outfitting of a weight and workout room.

We actively pursue such help from anyone and everyone who is able to contribute, and, in general, we've found that most people who've achieved success are ready and willing to give back to the broader community. We're grateful for their help.

Skewer the Principal

I had to let go one Spanish teacher who habitually failed 90 to 95 percent of her pupils. I believe in strict standards, but when only one child in ten is learning, I know it's not the fault of the kids! Nothing I or her department chairman said or did made any difference in this teacher's instructional methods. So I discontinued her particular course specialty on the basis of "inadequate enrollment"—which was true; kids did not sign up for her elective because they knew there was no chance of passing with her.

I thought that was the end of the story. Not quite.

On the evening of the Parents' Association meeting just after Ms. Suarez's departure, Peter Engel came to my office to say, "There are thirty-five or forty parents that I don't recognize in the teachers' cafeteria for the meeting tonight. I think they're here because of Ms. Gonzalez-Suarez."

There was nothing to do but face them. When I got to the teachers' cafeteria, it was indeed packed. The familiar parents were far outnumbered by people I had never seen before. The meeting began.

Once the principal's report was given and the regular agenda items were covered, a hand from the audience shot up. "I want to know—we want to know," a woman shouted, "why you fired Ms. Suarez for no good reason!" All the new people looked at her. Some of them were Latinos; they looked as though they weren't sure exactly what their English-speaking spokeswoman had said, although they certainly caught the basic drift. And then they looked at me, waiting for a response.

I don't know what made me do it, but I decided to respond in Spanish. Using my broken high school Spanish as best I could, I said, "*Lo siento mucho mi Español es muy pobre, pero la Señora Suarez no tiene un programa aquí porque nosotros no tenemos bastante estudiantes por ella aquí. Pero yo se que ella está trabajando en una otra escuela.*" ("I'm very sorry—my Spanish is very poor—but Ms. Suarez has no program here because we don't have enough students for her here. But I know that she is already working in another school.") All of this was strictly true, of course.

Most of the protestors were startled—as was my staff—that I knew a word of Spanish, bad as it was. They also looked surprised at the information about the inadequate student numbers and about Ms. Suarez's new employment. Several loudmouth die-hards started yelling questions about what I'd already explained, demanding information I didn't care to explain: "Why was she fired? Who took her place? Why are there not enough students?"

I had no intention of arguing with the group of hotheads with the cooler ones staying on to watch the "Skewer-the-Principal Show," so I said (in English this time), "I'm going to my office. Choose two or three people to come and speak with me about this matter." I turned on my heel and left as this message was being translated.

Fifteen minutes later, a delegation of three sat at my conference table with the door shut as I patiently went over what I had said. A small crowd of six or seven stood outside my door, waiting. The others had gone home.

Two or three of my stalwart assistant principals stayed around just in case anything bad happened. Nothing did. After twenty minutes or so, the delegation left. I assume that they had faithfully carried out their charge of "You go to that PA meeting and make that principal tell you why I got fired and see if you can scare her into letting me come back." No more was heard of the whole thing, and the newcomers never appeared at another Parents' Association meeting.

Thankfully, something had told me how to defuse the situation; in retrospect, we could have had a mob scene on our hands. That's not the way we wanted Taft to show up on the evening news!

"There's Hope Here!"

My staff was always ready to protect me from crazy parents. One day during my first month, as I was going down the hall to my office, Martin met me halfway and said, "Maybe you'd better not go to your office."

"Why?" I asked.

"Because there's a big, loud, angry woman there—Keith Maxwell's mom—and she looks like she's out for blood."

"It's okay," I said. "I come from a family of large, loud talkers." So I walked in, right past the woman as she sat fuming outside my door, and buzzed Irene MacKenzie, my secretary, to send her in. She burst into the room.

"Good afternoon," I greeted her. "Won't you have a seat?"

"No. I don't wanna sit down."

"Stand, then," I said, remaining in charge by this command. "How can I help you?"

"I want to know what kind of fuckin' school you got going here! Suspendin' my son! All he did was have a little fight in the lunchroom."

"That's a serious rule he broke," I replied. "And at Taft that calls for some time out, a suspension from school for some days."

"Time out!" she yelled. "That means time out *at home*! What am I gonna do with him at home? I don't want him home! That's why I came. I don't want him suspended."

"Just a minute," I said. I went to the phone and asked Irene, "Would you get Keith Maxwell's counselor to pull his permanent record card and bring it and Keith here?"

In the interim, I offered, "Mrs. Maxwell, would you like some tea or coffee?"

"No, thanks," she said, as she sat down.

I made myself some tea. The record card came before Keith did. I looked it over. "Mrs. Maxwell, the record shows that you've been coming to school for Keith since kindergarten, and he's been fighting since kindergarten. But his standard scores in reading and math are quite good. He's not a stupid boy—he's got good brains."

"You think I don't know that?" she said. "Teachers been telling me that for years. Been tellin' him, too, but he don't hear us—leastways he don't act it. He's smart about cuttin' school and hanging out!" Tears rolled silently down her big, round face.

I gave Keith's mom some tissues, which I always kept handy, and as she wiped her eyes and blew her nose, I poured her some coffee. "Cream?" I asked.

"No, black, two sugars," she replied. "What I'm gonna do with this boy? He's the oldest of my four boys—they all lookin' to him. His father's been done gone, and the streets is just grabbin' at him. I keep pullin' him back, but it's getting harder now he's seventeen."

"Let's get him in here," I said as I went to the door. "Come in, Keith, your mom's here."

A tall, handsome, well-muscled boy came in. I was glad to see that his face wasn't hardened and that he looked with a kind of respect and surprise at his mother being there; so often, the boys come in with "Who cares?" expressions of disdain and contempt, imitating the street boys they see around the neighborhood. I thought to myself, "There's hope here!"

"Keith," I said, "your mom and I have been reviewing your past. Parts of it look good, and parts don't. You're quite an intelligent boy—I mean, *young man*—although your grades don't reflect it. Actually, you're college material."

His face brightened at this. I continued. "What would you say if I told you that if you studied hard and broke sweat for the next months in our special GED program with Ms. Tobachnikoff, you could graduate at the same time as your class and go to Bronx Community College?"

"Is that possible—no joke, Ms. Monroe?"

"It is, but you have to really buckle down, come every day, do what Ms. Tobachnikoff says, and study at home every night. I know, with your brains, it's not 'Can you do it?' It's 'Will you do it?' So will you?"

"I'll try," he said.

I shook my head. "*Try* is not good enough. I want you to say *I will do it.*"

He said it—and in time, he did do it. After Keith left my office, his mother and I shared mother-of-teenage-boy stories. She left after giving me a big bear hug in the doorway, much to the amazement of the staff that was standing by—just in case.

Lost to the Streets

Only once did it prove necessary to have my staff standing by to prevent violence. One late winter day—it was February, I think—a Mr. William Ford came in to register his son, William, Jr., Willie for short. They had just moved into our school's zone from Philadelphia.

The father was gruff-voiced, with eyes that darted frequently toward the window: "Just watching my car," he said. He was scruffy, unkempt, and dirty, and so was the boy. They had no school records, just their word that Willie was an eleventh-grader. And since he was sixteen and a half years old, we guessed that that would be the appropriate placement for him, at least until the official records came.

In the following days, I had occasion to chat with Willie, who was amiable and quite eager to talk about his life with his father in Philly. Without my asking, he revealed that his father's occupation was car theft and that he'd often help his father in that line of work, which, he explained, "It's easy when you know how, and my pop knows how. Makes pretty good money at it, too, but mostly drinks it up. He told me, 'Let's go to New York for a change of scenery.' I think things were getting hot for him in Philly, so we're living with some cousins here in the Bronx."

Willie and I got along fine until his records came a week or so later. His counselor came to me and said, "Willie's records show that he has only three earned credits. He's really a ninth-grader. It's going to be hard to break the news to him, especially since his reading and math scores are too low for him to get into our GED program."

When Willie was told, he went berserk. "Oh, no! I ain't no ninth-grader, and I ain't going to be put in no ninth grade with them baby kids! I'm bigger than all of 'em—I'm bigger than most teachers! I ain't going. My pop'll take care of this! Y'all better watch out—he'll be in tomorrow."

Well, the next day, Willie didn't come to school. I was in my office at around four o'clock when in burst Willie Senior, holding his right hand behind his back.

"Sir," I said, strangely unafraid, "how can I help you?"

"Help? Yeah, you can help. Put Willie back in the eleventh grade where he belongs!"

"But he doesn't belong in the eleventh grade. He has only three credits."

"I don't care!" he bellowed. "Put him back, I say—put him back right now!"

Quietly I replied, "I can't and I won't."

At that, I saw his right hand come from behind his back. In it was a bicycle chain which he whipped over his right shoulder. I jumped back as the metal missed my face and landed with a crash on the desk.

This time, having my staff standing by was a godsend. Peter Engel and two security guards had seen Ford come into the building and heard him bellowing. They rushed in, and the two security guards grabbed him.

One said, "You want us to arrest him? We can, you know."

My first mind wanted to say, "Yeah, arrest him," but instead I said, "Listen, Mr. Ford. I'm not going to press charges. But if you ever come near or in the building again I will have you arrested. Do you understand me?"

He glowered and didn't respond.

"Do you understand me?" I repeated loudly, using my father's voice.

"Yes," he said as they escorted him out of the building.

"You all right?" Peter Engel asked.

"Yes," I said, "a little shaken, but all right." As I looked out of my window I saw Willie, Jr., leaning on a long, sleek black car waiting across the street for his dad. I never saw either of them again.

The Will to Win

Most people fear and abhor conflict. But if you are a leader of any group or aspire to a leadership role, you'll find yourself thrust into situations where battle is inevitable—if not physical battle, then psychological and emotional battle. Facing such challenges with strength and equanimity is a must.

As for me, I must admit that while I never look for a fight, once engaged I find that I enjoy the challenge. Somehow a reflexive response takes over, and my mind and body take on an attitude of "So, you want to fight, do you? I'm ready!" The adrenaline rush seems to give me not only the energy but also the words, deeds, and will I need to win.

On Leadership (II)

Don't be afraid to break rules, but do it only for the sake of the mission.

~

While working your tail off to accomplish Plan A, Always have Plans B and C written down somewhere—if need be, in code. And remember the code!

~

Spread the knowledge! The wisdom of any system must never reside in the head of a single person—not even you.

~

The leader who loses direct contact with the work loses perspective. The further you get from the work, the easier it is to promulgate nonsense.

~

A leader who plans, acts, walks, and talks like a leader—and wears a good suit—is damn near invincible!

~

The good leader knows that it's time to move on long before her followers.

CHAPTER 10

You Cannot Lose Your Good"

FINDING A NEW PATH—
TALES OF A ROVING EDUCATOR

Since about the eighth grade, I've always been a take-charge kind of person. I love to plan, organize, and make things happen. But no matter how well we plan, life has a way of surprising us. And surprises can be hard to take, especially when they come in the form of losses, hurts, disappointments, or tragedies.

Still, I've found that in all the ways that matter, the most worthwhile things in life never really go away. As I sometimes put it, "You cannot lose your good." When it seems you have lost your good, it is because your good has changed form. Your job is to learn to recognize its new shape.

Back in the ninth grade at J.H.S. 81, an all-girls junior high, I had the grand title of Head of Heads—chief officer in the School Patrol. I was in charge of an organization numbering nearly one hundred girls, with responsibility for inspecting their work, calling and running meetings, and recommending patrol members for promotions within the organization. It was a heady taste of leadership for someone not yet fifteen years old.

During the spring semester, I became ill and was out of school for some days. While I was out, senior class pins were distributed to all the ninth-graders. When I returned, my pin somehow was missing. Had someone stolen it? I was disturbed and upset at the idea, and I decided to investigate. So one day in class, when our fearsome teacher, Mrs. Graves, was out of the room, I stood up and asked if anyone knew what had happened to my pin.

What happened next stunned me. All of a sudden, I found myself in a kangaroo court made up of my classmates—girls I thought were my friends. My asking about the whereabouts of my pin became an occasion for the girls to direct an unexpected explosion of anger, resentment, and hard feelings toward me. "Who do you think you are?" one girl screamed. "You're not a teacher!" another yelled. And a third shouted, "You think you're hot stuff, don't you?" I was struck dumb by the intensity of the resentment, of which I had not even had the slightest inkling. I stood there staring at them, giving no answers, but I remember stubbornly thinking, "Yes, maybe I *am* hot stuff."

I went home, and when my mother came home from work, I told her about what had happened. My greatest pain, I told her, came not from the loss of the pin or the two or three most vicious outbursts, but from the fact that not one of my friends that I had known since the fourth grade had spoken up for me.

I'll always remember my mother's response. She said, "Don't be surprised at the girls' behavior: You'll meet people like this in your life as long as you're trying to succeed and do what you think is right." As for the silence of the ones I'd considered my friends, the loss of their voices—being forced to face the anger alone—was, as I think of it now, a strange gift. It was the gift of belief in myself and in my rightness, and the gift of resiliency to carry on as leader in the same ways that they had attacked me for.

Subsequently, I questioned myself about what happened in school that day. Had I been behaving arrogantly, in a way that might have explained—if not justified—my classmates' anger? As I've said, my leadership role felt like pretty heady stuff at the time. I can recall one instance when I behaved in a way I wish I hadn't. In a meeting, I referred to a particular student as "that Lawrence girl," which is how I'd heard teachers refer to students. The student overheard, and indignantly retorted, "Who are you calling 'that Lawrence girl'? You ain't my teacher!" I apologized, and I never spoke that way again—until years later, when I did indeed become a teacher.

But in general, I don't think I behaved arrogantly. I think I behaved as a leader. An effective leader can't be tentative or apologetic about making plans, setting a direction, or giving orders. And I certainly am not a tentative or apologetic person by nature, though I try hard not to do things I'll have to apologize for later.

In retrospect, I can understand why the girls I'd thought were my friends didn't rise to my defense: they were outnumbered and outpressured by their peers. Still, their failure to support me hurt. Among other things, the incident taught me how to handle criticism—to examine it, value what was true, and discard the rest. Not that this is easy to do. I used to spend a lot of time chewing over criticism and complaints, turning negative comments over and over in my mind. I'm faster now at sifting out the truth, and I move on faster, using my energy to plot new things instead of revisiting the past.

I find that when I have enemies, this behavior usually confounds them. Negative people get their jollies from watching the discomfort and anxiety they create in the people they attack. Best of all, they love to see a leader back down from a previous hard line that she took for the good of the organization. If you aspire to leadership, don't give in to this kind of pressure—if for nothing else, for the sake of your own spirit.

"I'm Only Connected to God"

I've learned that in your career and in your life, it pays to be prepared for the unexpected, both good and bad. No one can predict where any choice will ultimately lead. In that sense, everything we do is filled with risk. Choosing smart risks, and being prepared to live with the results, is a key to emotional and spiritual health.

Perhaps the riskiest career move I ever made was accepting an offer to serve as deputy chancellor in charge of curriculum and instruction under New York City schools chancellor Anthony Alvarado. I'd never heard of Alvarado until his name appeared in the *New York Times* at the time a new chancellor was being chosen in 1983, and we met for the first time when he interviewed me for the job as his deputy in May of '83. But I was excited by the prospect of transferring what I'd done at Taft to the larger arena of the entire New York City school system.

Looking back, I think my hopes were utterly naive. I've never worked such long, hard hours as I did during my time at 110 Livingston Street. But the sheer size of the school system, the myriad departments to be consulted, the layers of approval necessary, and the dozens of clashing constituencies to be wooed, cajoled, and mollified made it impossible to swiftly implement even the worthiest projects. When those obstacles didn't thwart progress, bureaucratic inertia would. For example, I thought that the successful in-school voter registration program implemented at Taft by Gerry Cioffi would be a worthy citywide project. I suggested this to the appropriate curriculum coordinator, who nodded, said, "Good idea!" and never acted on it.

I was stunned by the number of meetings I had to attend, and by how little was accomplished. Many meetings ended with no agreement on follow-up steps or actions to be taken. Some committees seemed to meet for the sole purpose of meeting.

The fact is, after my years as a successful principal, I was spoiled for work in the educational bureaucracy. I was used to being the boss. As principal, I could develop a creative idea, select staff members to implement it, support it, monitor it, evaluate its success, and move on. At 110, nothing was ever so simple or so satisfying. And I found that I missed the kids, too.

It didn't take long for me to realize that I didn't belong at 110 Livingston Street. Whatever the culture there was, I clearly didn't fit into it; in fact, I was never invited in. I was criticized for failing to hang out with the "in people" at 110, and that's probably true. After putting in my twelve-hour workdays, I chose to fulfill my family and other obligations rather than socialize with the politically connected crowd. Perhaps I would have helped my career had I done otherwise, but I don't regret my choice.

Ironically, the rumor around the school system was that I'd gotten my job at 110 because of my political connections: supposedly, I "knew somebody." Gossipmongers claimed that I'd known Chancellor Alvarado for years and had worked with him in School District 4. Neither statement was true.

Occasionally, bold people would ask me, "So, Lorraine, you have a great job at the Board of Ed. Whom do you know?" I'd answer flippantly, "Nobody except God." That got me quite a few funny looks. But it was true.

Shortly before I was let go by the Board of Ed, a board member whom I knew only slightly asked me to lunch at Gage & Tollner's, a fine old restaurant in Brooklyn. Politically naive as I was, even I knew enough to accept a lunch invitation from a board member. After we'd chatted a while, the board member remarked, "Tell me, Lorraine, how did you get chosen for your job?"

Honestly, I replied, "I really don't know. I guess the chancellor had heard of my work at Stevenson and Taft."

She persisted. "Did you know the chancellor from District 4?"

"No," I replied.

"And are you connected with any politicians in Brooklyn?"

"No," I said, and I added my usual disclaimer, "I'm only connected to God." She smiled, and we ordered coffee.

Only later, after I'd been dismissed from the job, did I understand the purpose of the lunch invitation. Her job had been to find out whether firing me would provoke any political uproar. My answers had convinced her, correctly, that it wouldn't.

When One Door Closes, Another Opens

Being fired from my job as deputy chancellor was the career loss that knocked me for the greatest loop. In 1984, Chancellor Alvarado, who had been responsible for hiring me, resigned from his post, to be replaced by Nathan Quiñones. I knew intellectually that the chancellor's staff served at his pleasure. I assumed, however—somewhat naively—that since I had done good work, I would remain in my position under the new chancellor.

I was in for a rude awakening. After a meeting with Mr. Quiñones and his new deputy, Chuck Schonhaut, not only was I not retained, but Mr. Quiñones also sent me a letter thanking me for my efforts, summarily ordering me back to my old post as principal at Taft, and giving me one day in which to be packed and out of the building!

I was stunned at this treatment. I had to read the letter twice to fully understand what it said. Dazed, I moved through the day feeling as if I were walking through deep water. How could I break the news to my family, who were so proud of me? More important, what could I tell myself? What sense did my firing make? I knew I wasn't incompetent. I also wasn't politically ambitious. Had I alienated or threatened someone, somehow? Should I have handled my job differently? If so, how?

In time, I shook off the questions and the self-doubts. Maybe there were things I could have done to fit in better with the system at 110, but I knew in my heart of hearts that I didn't want to change. I believe too fully in who I am and in my style of educating and leading. If the price I had to pay was being fired, so be it.

But I also knew that as much as I'd loved being principal of Taft and as good as the staff and I had done there, I was not going back. I intended only to go forward wherever forward was. Numb but determined, I sat and planned on paper my next steps. I used up most of my sick time and continued my doctoral work at Teachers College at Columbia University. Ultimately, I took a year's leave for study, finished my doctorate in June of 1985, and moved on to full-time teaching in graduate school—a dream I'd long held. More surprising, I then moved into national and international consulting—a dream I'd never had.

Ironically, at the time of Chancellor Alvarado's departure, if I'd been offered almost any job at the Board of Ed, I probably would have taken it. I would have continued to put in punishing hours, trying desperately to make a difference in the citywide school system, fighting against overwhelming odds and stifling inertia. But as a friend at Bank Street College told me, "If you stay inside, nobody outside will ever know you or even know you're looking for a greater opportunity."

I see now that the loss of my job in the Board of Ed bureaucracy opened up possibilities for me that would never have opened if I had stayed at 110 Livingston Street in any capacity. It makes me appreciate the wisdom in the biblical tale of Joseph and his brothers. Maybe you remember the story: Joseph, beloved by his father, Jacob, was envied and hated by his brothers. They sold him into slavery, but he rose to power in Egypt and was able to help not only his brothers, who had betrayed him, but all the people of Israel: "You meant it for evil, but God meant it for my good."

In times of difficulty, I remember Joseph's words and ask myself, "Why is this happening to me?" A quiet voice answers, "In time, it will become clear." In time, it does.

"It's a Miracle!"

Today I spend the greater part of my time as a consultant to schools and school systems around the world, and some small part of my time counseling women. My "consulting" career really started with what might be called career coaching. Women who knew me and noticed my ability and willingness to speak out and be heard—as you know by now, I'm not exactly a wallflower—began to come to me for help with their personal communication and leadership skills. I helped them revise their résumés and put them through mock interviews. I'm proud to say that every person I ever coached got the job she wanted.

One case was really tough: the woman was so wooden, so lacking in self-confidence in voice, spirit, and posture that I truly did not believe she could get through a job interview successfully. We had three long sessions of really brutal criticism and practice. On a physical level, I had her practice walking, shaking hands, maintaining eye contact, and varying her voice, all to help her make a stronger impression when she walked into the interview.

More important, on a psychological level, I worked with her to recognize and speak about the full, accomplished life that she had led as opposed to what her résumé indicated. We'd speak about her life and work, and like many of the women I've worked with, she'd casually mention something truly interesting and impressive that she'd done. I'd ask, "Why didn't you put that on your résumé?" She'd answer, "Oh, I didn't think that was important." Seeing my reaction helped her realize how much she'd really achieved. She learned to express these personal strengths more forcefully, and in the end she got the job.

Another tough case I took on involved a woman who had not finished, and seemingly *could* not finish, her master's thesis. I was her third coach. The woman was smart and had a real knowledge of her subject, but coherence escaped her. It was painfully hard for her to explain anything sequentially. The only solution, we discovered, was to work together on her thesis, hammer and tongs, for countless sessions, section after section.

I'd point to a sentence in her draft manuscript and ask, "What do you mean by this?"

She'd say, "I mean . . ." and she'd explain it quite clearly.

"Fine," I'd say. "Don't say another word—just write down what you just told me. And what logically comes next?"

"Why, thus-and-so."

"Now write *that*. And what do you conclude from this?"

"I conclude this and that."

"Then write that now . . ." And this is the way we went through the entire thesis.

A month after our final session, she came to my office with a bunch of flowers for me. Her thesis had been approved. We laughed, cheered, and hugged. After she left, two colleagues asked me what all the noise was about. To their amazement, I fell to the floor laughing and rolled over several times. "What is it, Lorraine?" one asked. "Get up, crazy!" said the other. I got up, crying, "It's a miracle, a miracle! She finished her thesis!" I knew I was a pretty good writing teacher, but until that moment I hadn't known the tension I'd been under, working with her week after week.

I never again undertook to help a student write or rewrite a thesis.

Shaking Loose Entrenched Attitudes

In 1985, I began to work as a paid consultant. It started when an acquaintance, Kathie Lane, insisted that I get business cards. Previously, when people sought me out at conferences and meetings, I had jotted my name and telephone number on restaurant napkins and scraps of paper. I had also been advising people for very little money or no money at all. Perhaps there was cause-and-effect at work here! At Kathie's prodding, three days before flying off to the International Women's Conference in Nairobi, I rushed to the local copy center and got cards made up.

At the conference, I gave my first card out to a woman who wanted to change her life and job. When we came back to New York City, I met with her and helped her think out loud about her hopes and future. She left our session feeling confident that she wasn't crazy to want to change and realizing that she had accumulated a lot of skills. She was ready to take a well-thought-out risk.

While teaching at Bank Street College, I worked mainly as a consultant in middle schools in New York City. Then, in the summer of 1989, I happened to be in my office at B.S.C. when the phone rang. I wasn't going to answer it, because I was supposed to be on vacation, but something made me pick it up anyway. It was a person I'd met once in Indiana when I was on a panel for the Lily Foundation. He asked me whether I'd like to join a team of consultants traveling across the United States on behalf of the Edna McConnell Clark Foundation, who were interested in funding some worthwhile middle school initiatives. I eagerly agreed, because I love to travel, and boy, do I love to talk about education!

Hayes Mizell, the director of the initiative, later called me, and I accepted formally. I joined a group of three incredibly talented, fun consultants, and we formed a great team. Those experiences and presentations across the country increased my consultancies to a point where 80 percent of my work took me out of New York City.

For nearly four years, I traveled the country and met wonderful educators. When I talked to teachers, they would say, "My principal needs to hear you." When I talked to principals, they'd say, "My teachers need to hear you." So whenever I could, I spoke to both. I also worked with principals and teachers in middle schools in three districts in Manhattan.

Consulting gave me an opportunity to share my ideas about education and leadership with a wide array of people, and to meet and help people struggling with the challenges of education at many different levels of commitment and competency.

Once I was asked to consult with a group of teachers whose principal had designated them as top-drawer. Most of the group was cooperative and lively, and we had a wonderfully productive session. But one teacher sat glowering and looking altogether resentful and absent. The only words she uttered during our long group sessions were "I'm listening" or "I have no comment." In private, she told me with a penetrating glare, "I've been teaching a *long* time." I suppose I was meant to finish the sentence with, "And I know everything." What a lost opportunity for her to learn something new!

In this same group was a woman who, when I said, "Let's talk about planning and the ways that you lay out your semester's work," said blithely, "I never plan; I just let things happen."

"Really?" I replied. "How long have you been teaching?"

"Fifteen years," she answered.

I was stunned. I tried hard to control my voice and my eyebrows as I said, "Let me show you how I plan, because I think it's essential to effective teaching." She looked amazed and said nothing—but she took notes.

I visited another school in which the principal was attempting to attract "middle-class kids" (often a euphemism for "white kids" in a minority-dominated neighborhood). The principal identified four star teachers who were working with a group of eighth-graders. The conversation turned to what seemed to be effective with their particular kids. One teacher who was a bit haughty in attitude and very self-assured blurted out, "Well, I'll tell you what's *not* effective—teaching these kids fractions. It's hopeless! They don't get it. So I've stopped trying to teach fractions. Besides, they don't need fractions in their lives."

I couldn't believe my ears. I confess, I lost control. I stood up and said, "They don't need fractions in their lives? They don't need fractions? They *live* fractions! Their hat and shoe sizes are fractions! A slice of bread is a fraction! A piece of pizza is a fraction!" My voice escalated to a yell. "A potato chip is a fraction, half an apple is a fraction, a piece of cake is a fraction! Teachers say, 'Fold your paper in half,' and the kids know what to do—they *know* fractions! *Your job is to make them see that they already know fractions!*"

She was stunned by my loss of cool, as were the other teachers. I think she was also ashamed. I calmed down, and we went back to talking about how to set challenging assignments for kids—including teaching fractions.

I continued to work with this school, and as I did, I observed a fascinating phenomenon. As more challenging classroom work became the rule, more "middle-class" parents and parents aspiring to become middle-class began to enroll their children there. Before this new influx of parents arrived, teachers and counselors had complained, "Oh, if we only had more parental involvement! We call for parents to visit, and they don't come. I don't think many of them care. If they did, we could do so much more with their kids."

The next year, I was amazed to hear the *opposite* lament voiced against the "upwardly mobile" parents: "These new parents are such busybodies. They're always coming into school, questioning everything. It's so time-consuming explaining things to them!"

Rediscovering What You Already Know

Quite often, the work of the consultant is simply to point out things that are obvious. Training educators to step back from a situation in order to see it clearly is a simple common sense technique. In one school, I was working with a group of four teachers who had been identified as teachers who were amenable to change. They taught a group of seventh-graders who had been retained—"left back"—three times. In the course of our conversations, I said that I believed homework was necessary for reviewing and reinforcing work done in school, and there was general agreement that a homework policy was important.

One teacher then volunteered that she had made a rule that three missing homeworks meant failure for her students. Before I could question her policy, she said, "Let me give you an example. I've got this kid, José—he's homeless. He sleeps on the subway or wherever he can every night, and he never does his homework."

"Hmm," I said. "Let me repeat what you've just said to me: 'He's homeless, he sleeps on the subway, and he doesn't do his homework.'"

She stared at me blankly. "Suppose I say it three times," I offered. (The Jesuits say that if you teach someone something three times, they are sure to learn it.) So I repeated her words three times, and each time I emphasized the words "homeless" and "homework."

After the third time, the light clicked on. She said, "Oh, he has no *home* to do *home*work in!"

"Right!" I replied. "So let's all spin a couple of alternatives:

"(1) He can do homework before school, after school, at lunchtime in your room, or in the school media center. Or,

"(2) He can go to the nearby library and do homework there until closing time if necessary."

She was pleased with these alternatives, and when I returned some weeks later and asked about José's progress, she smiled and said, "He's doing his work now."

"Great!" I said. But immediately her expression changed. "Why, what's wrong? You look displeased."

"I still don't feel right about it," she replied. "I feel like a chump because he's getting over on me by not doing homework at home like the rest of the kids."

There was nothing I could say to convince her except "Be thankful— he's doing the work." School traditions die hard.

Another time, a colleague and I were asked by a school superinten- dent to visit his district in Connecticut to help the staff figure out how to get their "ninety-nine black underachievers" (as they put it) to suc- ceed academically. We were given ten two-hour sessions in which to accomplish this.

Before we started, I knew what the problem was. The trick would be to get the school administrators we were working with to see it for themselves.

Session after session, my colleague and I talked with the administra- tors about past successes that they'd enjoyed with white students. They described the obstacles they'd had to overcome when working with "white underachievers," as well as the methods and personnel they'd used to achieve those successes.

At the end of the eighth session, one of the administrators raised his hand and asked the question we'd been waiting for: "Do you suppose that we should do for our *black* underachievers what worked with our *white* underachievers?"

It took all of my composure to answer quietly, "I think it's worth a try."

We then spent the last two sessions blocking out what needed to be done for which kids and what resources to apply. Later that year, the superintendent reported that his "black underachievers" had raised their test scores to a remarkable degree.

Another story about seeing the obvious: I was asked to help a middle school math teacher who was having discipline problems. I visited his classroom. "Sit in on the next class," he suggested. "Then you'll see why I can't teach these kids."

I watched the chaos: kids were talking, laughing, and walking around the room, completely ignoring the teacher, who was delivering instruction to the few kids struggling to listen over the noise.

Finally, the bell rang, and the kids tumbled out of the room. "Do you have another class coming in?" I asked.

"No, thank God!" he replied. "So now you see why I can't teach!"

"Yes," I replied. "I do see. What do you think would help you become effective with these children?"

"Well," he said, "I'll tell you. If I knew whether there was a father in the home, or if the mother worked, or if the brothers and sisters were on crack cocaine . . . "

I interrupted the litany. "If you knew these things, how would that help you get them seated and quiet in class?"

He wrinkled his brow. "I don't know," he admitted.

"I don't know, either," I said. "So instead, let me help you with some simple opening routines that don't require you to get their attention by talking." I outlined several basic rules for getting a class organized and working during the first five minutes of the period, and he agreed to try them. After a few weeks, he had taken control of his class and was able to begin real teaching.

What Color Are the Winners?

One kindergarten teacher with a class full of homeless children living in hotel rooms lamented, "I have a problem." She sounded exasperated. "These children come in in the morning, and they're so restless and active. All they want to do is run up and down the hall! I want to start skill building first thing and then around ten a.m. go outside for recess, but the first thing they want to do is run and run."

I asked, "Do you know the conditions in which the children live?"

"No," she confessed.

"They live in hotel rooms with their mothers and brothers and sisters. The streets and the hotel halls are dangerous, because illicit happenings and dangerous people are everywhere. So the kids are confined to the rooms for hours at a time for their protection. By the time they come to school, they *need* to run—they're normal kids! Why not reverse your schedule? Plan to have recess first. It could even be "structured recess," with counting and running games, ABCs, and ball games. Then do concrete skill building later."

"That's a good idea," she conceded. "I'll try it. But it's going to be strange, because recess *always* comes at ten."

I visited another school and was proudly shown around by the principal. Over one classroom door was a sign, "In this room are the winners."

"Can we go in there?" I asked. "I want to see the winners." When I entered, I noticed that all the "winners" were white kids—even though I had noticed quite a number of children of color in the building. I also looked at the work they were doing, and I saw that the students were working on nonchallenging, meaningless "drill and kill" sheets—hardly challenging, inspiring stuff.

When we left the room, I said to the principal, "I noticed that all the kids in there are white. Why are there no black or brown winners?"

He said without skipping a beat, "They're not qualified." And without thinking I replied, "Then *make* them qualified!"

I was appalled at his coolness and lack of embarrassment in the face of my being there, and I felt deeply sad for the kids both black and white. They were being taught false, life-destroying lessons regarding their superiority and inferiority.

One school where I was asked to work over time had a large number of special education classes, mainly made up of boys. After I'd observed several classes where nothing academically challenging ever happened, one boy confided to me, "You know something, Dr. Monroe? I'm only 'special ed' here in school. Around my block and in my family, nobody knows and thinks I'm special ed."

What a tragic comment. Think of what was *not* being expected of him or done for him. For that boy, school was just a place—the *only* place—where he was pulled down by the stigma of failure.

There was one very sad, totally nonfunctional school that I worked at for a time. The school was in utter chaos: low staff morale, low student achievement, violence among kids, vandalism. Whenever I visited, I had to make my way through crowds of kids loitering in the halls. At the principal's request, I sat in on "School-Based Management" committee meetings—a current fad—where most staffs meet and meet and meet and do nothing. Although the faculty and staff all said they wanted order and structure in the school, no one seemed willing to do anything except meet and talk about how bad conditions were. I stopped going to the meetings.

I continued to meet with the principal, however, sharing with her some techniques I had used to bring order to similarly chaotic schools. She smiled, took notes, and thanked me, but week after week I saw no progress. Finally, one week when I came, she greeted me with a broad grin and said, "Come, Dr. Monroe. I want to show you my latest innovation."

She escorted me upstairs, where I expected to go into a classroom. Instead, we turned left to the second-floor girls' bathroom. She threw open the door grandly. "See," she said as she pointed to a table under a mirror, on which were placed a supply of facial tissues, hand lotion, sanitary napkins, and tampons. She beamed as she said, "For the girls' comfort."

I said nothing, and she opened the door onto the hallway filled with boys and girls—obviously quite "comfortable"—who were shouting and running up and down. I left and called the superintendent to tell him that I could not return to that school, because the leadership was hopeless.

The Kids Believe What They See

My work as a teacher at the Bank Street College of Education in New York overlaps quite a bit with what might be called consulting; I am often asked during or after class to help think through a problem that educators at a particular school are struggling with. One time, a coordinator of student activities at a high school said to me, "I need your help. I teach in an integrated school. But all the basketball players are African-American, and all the cheerleaders are white. I want to integrate the cheerleaders, but no black or Latina girls come to tryouts. What do you suggest?"

I asked, "How do you announce the tryouts?"

She replied, "I put up posters, pass out flyers, and make announcements over the public address system."

I thought those ought to work. But then it hit me. "Wait a minute," I said. "Do you have pictures of past and present teams and cheerleader squads hanging in your halls? And in those pictures, are all the cheerleaders white?"

"Yes," she replied.

"Then I think the kids believe the pictures. You have to go to all the homeroom classes and say forthrightly that you want to integrate the cheerleaders and that you will hold tryouts open until this happens."

Later she reported back. "I tried it, and it worked. The black girls told me that they didn't feel that they would be accepted as cheerleaders, since the school tradition seemed to be that the cheerleaders had always been white."

I'm a staunch advocate of change in schools, but change for its own sake can do more harm than good. It is very dangerous for some principals to go off to workshops and seminars, because they often bring back good practices and make every teacher adopt them—ready or not, trained or not. For example, they announce that "cooperative learning" (student group work) will be the new regime, not realizing that this technique is a very dangerous tool in the hands of teachers who have no idea of classroom control.

Other principals may glom on to a practice that has little or nothing to do with academic achievement ("We're going to put our chairs in a circle"). I knew one principal who drove an effective teacher quite mad by rearranging her room each evening when she left, changing the seat arrangement from six straight rows to a large circle. It even came to the point where the teacher would double back to school at odd times after 4:00 p.m. to monitor and replace her chairs. This particular principal was relatively ineffective as a school leader, but chair placement was one thing she could control!

It All Comes Back to Leadership

As a consultant, I can do a lot: suggest new ideas, generate a sense of excitement, tell inspiring stories, and remind people of the mission of the organization. But leadership is the key to school change. The leader needs to indicate daily, by word and deed:

❑ that our work is about transforming children's lives, every day

❑ that the work takes whatever it takes

❑ that no one way is The Way. The Way is any way that works, and the more ways you know, the more effective you are.

And the leader needs to send the message "I am here to support you in whatever way you choose, as long as your way improves children's academic and social achievement."

If every school had a leader like this, our kids and our communities would be in much better shape. I have consulted in schools across the country where:

- ❑ The principal lives in his/her office;
- ❑ The principal takes no risks because of the desire for approval or promotion;
- ❑ The principal allows racist behavior and practice;
- ❑ The principal is unknown to the students;
- ❑ The principal has no clue as to what is going on upstairs or right outside his/her door;
- ❑ The principal reads every piece of mail, every memo, and every fax, and doesn't delegate minutiae;
- ❑ The principal is paranoid ("Everyone is out to get me!");
- ❑ The principal doesn't have regular staff meetings;
- ❑ The principal has an "open-door policy," sees everybody indiscriminately, and has no ladder of referral—meaning that all problems go straight to him/her;

and, last but not least:

- ❑ The principal doesn't realize that without order no learning can take place.

A school saddled with a nonleader like this is unlikely to change for the better until the principal retires.

This Is School

Happily, as a consultant, I did have the opportunity to witness some wonderful educational experiences unfold. There was the remarkable teacher who invited me to see her Dance Program, done to celebrate Black History Month (February). When I arrived, the auditorium was already filled with noisy seventh- and eighth-graders—a tough audience. The curtains opened to reveal a line of female dancers, all in white tutus. And in the middle of the line was a very stout girl who stood out from the other middle-adolescent string beans.

The audience tittered and guffawed, but then the music began, and the girls danced, all in perfect synchronicity. The laughter stopped, as the kids were won over by the seriousness and loveliness of the dance and music. When the dance ended, there was loud applause.

I wept to see and hear what had happened. I thought how brave this teacher was to allow the fat girl to dance. Like so many other teachers, I would have been tempted to offer her a job as a curtain puller, program distributor, or usher. But this teacher understood, and I think she taught both the students and the adults a lesson: in this school, if you come out and make the audition and rehearsals, you dance. This is not Radio City Music Hall, and these are not the Rockettes. This is school, a place where the rigorous, even cutthroat competition of the outside world sometimes needs to be modified. *School should not reflect what society is, but rather school should model what society should be.*

On the Human Touch

Always put people first, paper second.

≈

Make yourself visible to those you want to influence—
every day, every way.

≈

Understanding and sympathy must go along with expecting and demanding the best. *Stroking* must accompany
poking.

≈

The good leader doesn't see or hear everything. Learn
what to ignore.

≈

Remember what people did to help and nurture you?
Do it for others.

≈

A leader who expects the best from everybody usually
gets it.

CHAPTER 11

Feed Your Soul

WHAT A LEADER MUST DO
TO NOURISH HER OWN SPIRIT

As I've mentioned, one of my favorite activities—and, I think, one of my most important—is traveling around the country, speaking to groups of educators and other professionals about my experiences in helping kids to learn and teachers to teach. I'll generally give a talk, tell some stories, and field questions from the audiences about my educational philosophy and methods. Quite often, however, someone—generally a woman—will stand up to ask a question that has nothing directly to do with teaching. It usually goes something like this: "Lorraine, as a working wife and mother, how do you manage to do all the things you do without getting worn out or discouraged?"

Because I think that this question is so important, I want to devote this chapter to answering it.

As I've gotten older and wiser, I've learned that I need to take care of myself—to "do for myself"—if I hope to take care of and do for others. It took me a while to understand this, because nurturing oneself can be seen as being selfish. But it isn't selfish—it's a simple necessity. You can't give to others what you don't have. To be an example or a model to others of health—of physical and mental vitality—means knowing first how to care for yourself.

Here are some of the lessons I've learned about self-nurturing over the years:

When you are working as a leader, you are in a role that is terribly demanding—physically, emotionally, mentally. It's crucial to have a life outside of your work to save your sanity: a life centered around family, friends, hobbies, or other work.

You need a confidant away from work, someone with whom you can laugh, shout, and cry. This need for emotional release is something you can't indulge on the job, but satisfying it at home or at play will strengthen you at the times when you must retain your self-control.

It also helps if you live with someone who understands what it means to be a leader—who understands why you are preoccupied with your mission. The real leader is always deeply involved in the life of the organization—thinking about new things, rethinking old ones, dreaming, planning, scheming. This happens on weekends, on vacation, early in the morning, and in the middle of the night. The ideal supporter is a person who loves you and understands and accepts this preoccupation as an essential aspect of who you are. And he or she will also know when and how to gently draw you away from thinking about work, when that is what you need the most!

Feeding Body and Soul

It's important to take care of yourself physically, starting with the foods you eat. I've learned to love eating whole grains, brown rice, fruits, and vegetables, and to appreciate the flavor of foods baked and broiled. This was a harder lesson than you might think. The way we eat is something we grow up with, and in my family the custom demanded frying almost everything—even cabbages and apples! Oh, I can't deny the deliciousness of Southern soul food, and on occasion I still feel driven to fix and eat those traditional fried delicacies, but I've learned to go back to enjoying healthy foods with the same delight.

Periodically I also go on fasts or semifasts, taking a day or two on a weekend to drink only herbal teas and juices and eat yogurt. In this way, I feel I can clear out my system of any poisons I may have accumulated in weeks of rushed or less-than-optimum eating.

I don't exercise as often as I'd like, but luckily I'm not inclined to putting on lots of weight. Maybe it's because I walk so fast. Hey, I do *everything* fast. When I was a child, my father once told me, "Lorraine, you always *go at* things," by which he meant that I move fast, doing things quickly—maybe too quickly, sometimes. I remembered his comment years later when someone asked me that familiar question, "How can you do all the things you do?" The answer is, I just go ahead and *do* them. I go at everything with quickness and with what may seem to the casual observer to be not much thought. But the truth is that I've usually thought a long time about what I want to do before I "go at" it.

The counterpart to doing things quickly is knowing how to relax—completely. I can sleep anywhere: on a train or plane, in a car, or in a hotel room anywhere in the world. I recently visited a spa with the intention of unwinding and comforting myself physically and psychologically after a period of intense activity. While there, I realized something about my physical being: although I can relax every part of my body by willing it to happen, it takes extra concentration to relax my neck and head. Maybe it's because that's (literally) my headquarters for thinking, planning, dreaming—the place where my restless spirit is usually active at all hours of the day and night.

Being in or around water is crucial for my sense of well-being. It's at the sea that I can most fully relax, let go, and meditate. When I can't go to the ocean, a bathtub works almost as well. Recently I traveled to another city to give a talk, and in order to relax before speaking I took a tub soak meditation in my hotel room. Before I knew it, I found myself coming out of a water-induced trance to answer the ringing phone. It was the hotel operator: "Dr. Monroe, Ms. Mack is here in the lobby, waiting to take you to your appointment" (keynote address)!

Sheepishly, I said to the operator, "Tell Ms. Mack I'll be down in ten minutes. I've been held captive in the tub!"

Controlling the Calendar

To nurture one's spirit also requires time—time to recharge the batteries and to escape the demands our work and our lives put on us. Just doing something—anything—to get away from other people can help. I go to the movies a lot, and I love listening to music.

I've also developed some unusual techniques for controlling my on-the-job schedule. When I worked at the New York City Board of Education, I found myself putting in twelve-hour days on a regular basis. I could deal with this physically, but my mind began to numb out from the intense pace. So I started inventing mythical appointments for myself. I would write into my calendar half-hour meetings with people who did not exist. This guaranteed me at least a half hour of free time to think, to have a cup of herbal tea, or just to breathe.

Of course, for the benefit of my secretary I had to maintain the charade. So I'd express disappointment over the nonexistent people who never kept their appointments, and she in turn would shake her head and complain about these unprofessional people: "Talk about rude! They make appointments with you and don't show up or even bother to call!"

I also try to keep part of each week and each year sacred, not letting work activities steal all my time and energy. I try to hold Friday night, all day Saturday, and part of Sunday for myself. I advise people who are striving to balance work and life to do the same—or to set aside other times. As an educator, I try to avoid working all through the summer. (If you're not a teacher, you may find this surprising, but it would be easy for me as a consultant to work straight through July and August and arrive at the new school year in September exhausted and tense.) I set aside early August as refueling time. For you, it may be a different time of year, but don't get into the habit of skipping vacations. Your spirit will suffer, and so will your work.

It also helps to know what you *hate* to do. Refuse to do it, except when you can't avoid it. Here's my list:

❏ Defrosting the refrigerator. (In my home, it can wait—at least until the freezer compartment door simply won't close any longer.)

❏ Cleaning the oven. (This one can wait *forever*. I have a theory that a layer of burned-on charcoal helps hold the heat.)

❏ Dusting the furniture. (I believe that dust forms a protective coating which helps furniture last longer.)

❏ Straightening out drawers and closets. (That's why they have doors.)

And, most important:

❏ Associating with negative people. (Once you're past the age of thirty, life is just too short to waste with whiners, drainers, and complainers.)

Journaling as Therapy

You also need to learn what kind of psychological or spiritual therapy works for you—what kinds of activities can help you to knit yourself back together when you unravel. For me, keeping a journal or diary plays an important role. I developed this habit when I first became a school administrator, partly as a way of releasing the pressures and tensions of my newfound leadership role. My journal became a place where I could dump my anxieties and worries, examine honestly my own strengths and weaknesses, curse my enemies, give thanks for my friends, make my plans for the organization, and in time, make my plans for *leaving* the organization. In my journal I could express thoughts and feelings that I could not share with colleagues, friends, or relatives. In fact, I wrote part of the journal in code, just in case it ever fell into "the wrong hands."

To this day, I periodically use my journal as a tool for making meaning from the present and for planning my futures. Yes, that's "futures" with an *s*. I expect to have several futures. I love to plan my tomorrows; after all, planning is a form of structured daydreaming, a way of giving shape to our hopes and desires, and I find it wonderfully energizing both personally and professionally. I believe that it's because I find joy in planning that I can energize others.

In Touch with the Spirit

O f course, the ultimate source of strength is God. Much as I love to plan and control things, much as I enjoy being the boss and making things happen the way I want, I'm well aware that no one can completely control her destiny. Everything we do is affected in a hundred big and small ways by factors we can't manipulate. Accepting this is crucial to inner peace.

In fact, I've found that I am most effective in life and work at the times when I am *not* entirely in control—at the times when a greater force is giving me the words and ideas I need. As a result, I've developed the habit of praying before any important meeting, speech, or work, appealing to the Holy Spirit like this: "Dear God, please help me to say and do the right things, so that someone here will be moved to do the work you have in mind for us to do."

I often recall a line from the poem "Housewifery," by Edward Taylor, a seventeenth-century poet: "Make me, O Lord, thy spinning-wheel complete." I understand and appreciate the idea of being a creative tool in the hands of God. Many hymns and spirituals express the same notion, and recalling them has often given me sustaining strength. The line from the old hymn "Here I am, Lord; send me" is an example. Another is the beautiful spiritual "Climbing Jacob's Ladder," whose message is that the work of God is progressive, to be done one small step at a time. It's a lesson I need to recall whenever I'm faced with a seemingly overwhelming task.

Combating Burnout

Feeling burnt-out—physically, emotionally, intellectually, and spiritually exhausted—is not uncommon among women (and men) who do work that is unfulfilling, unchallenging, or unrewarding. Caring for others without feeling cared-for yourself is one recipe for burnout. Another is remaining too long in a work or life situation that drains and batters you rather than feeding and uplifting you. In my work I've met many women who feel trapped in such situations.

What are the causes that lead women to feel unable to break free of a debilitating work environment? Here are a few that I've observed:

❑ They believe they lack the educational credentials, experience, or skills to change their work or careers.

❑ They overestimate the difficulty of making a break with their current situation.

❑ They lack confidence in their own talents and abilities.

❑ They receive little or no encouragement from the important people in their lives—spouses, parents, children, friends.

❑ They see only men, or only white people, or only highly educated people, or only some other seemingly privileged group doing the work to which they aspire.

❑ They feel they are too old to change.

❑ They're afraid of failing.

For over a decade, I've met with and counseled women (and some men) who have been hampered by such circumstances, and I've found that the key to helping them is much like the key to being an effective classroom teacher. The student—or in this case, the person seeking counsel—knows more than she thinks she knows. My job is to bring out what she knows by asking the right questions. Questions like:

❑ Who were you when you were a little girl? What did you dream of doing when you grew up?

❑ What happened to that dream? Are you living it now? If not, why not?

❑ What are you doing with your life today? How did you come to do this?

❑ If you are discontented with your life, why?

❑ Do you have a new dream today? If so, what is it?

❑ What would it take to achieve your new dream?

❑ What talents and strengths do you have that can help you pursue your dream? What obstacles could stand in your way?

❑ How have you used your talents and strengths to solve problems and overcome obstacles in the past? How can you use these same talents in pursuit of your dream?

Step by step, questions like these encourage a woman to explore the possibilities hidden in her own mind and spirit. Gradually, the image of a new path in life, filled with the potential for change and growth, begins to emerge.

However, taking the first few steps on a new path is a daunting challenge for many, especially for those who have been beaten down for years by difficult circumstances. When counseling someone, I often give her "homework assignments" between sessions. These assignments involve taking small personal risks, daring to do something she has been afraid to do in the past. Typical assignments include:

❑ Meditating or exercising—self-nurturing activities that can help lay the foundation for finding a new direction in life

❑ Saying no to a loved one's request that would encroach on your personal time

❑ Refusing to internalize a negative "You-can't-do-that" message or comment

❑ Signing up for a weekend or evening course or seminar to explore a path toward your dream

❑ Not revealing your plans or hopes for the future to anyone prematurely

❑ Taking time to be alone without apologies or explanations to anyone

❑ Practicing positive self-talk: "I can do it!"

❑ Buying yourself an enjoyable and *impractical* gift: flowers, perfume, fancy bath oil, or soap

❑ Recording in a journal what you do, think, and feel each day

If you find yourself in a potential burnout situation, try the questions and exercises I've suggested. Above all, realize that you *can* find and follow a better path. Many, many others have done so with no more resources than you possess.

Learning to Dream

Earlier in this book, I spoke about my family's influence on me. I can see now that I learned a great deal about nurturing and energizing myself from both my parents and my parents' parents. From their varied personalities and styles I've pieced together a way of living different from any of theirs, that I've found works for me. I was a lucky kid to have such different parents to contribute to who I am.

Twelve Ways I Feed My Spirit

1. Meditate.

2. Visit my therapist—the ocean—as often as possible.

3. Go to the movies to compare my taste to that of the voters for the Academy Awards. (We rarely agree.)

4. Carve out time to love my husband, children, and grandchildren.

5. Buy a new blouse.

6. Paint lots of things yellow.

7. Play Skee-Ball in the nearest arcade.

8. Drive my car fast by myself.

9. Shop for fresh fruits and vegetables, then take them home to cook and savor them while talking and laughing with friends and family.

10. Browse in a good bookstore.

11. Stretch out in front of a roaring fire, reading and listening to Bach.

12. Pray for peace, strength, and guidance.

On Inner Strength

Sometimes it will feel as though the world's mission is to wear you down! Good work is *not* for the faint of heart.

～

When the leader who is right knuckles under to the protests of the incompetent, she is knuckled into failure.

～

For a time, you can run on Empty physically—but only if you're charged up spiritually.

～

Formula for victory: First you pray, then you work.

CHAPTER 12

Last Licks

SOME THINGS I'VE LEARNED

ABOUT MYSELF AND THE WORK

Writing this book has been for me a time of reflection and looking back. Thinking about my life, from my earliest childhood days till now, and about the work I've done in and around schools, has brought home to me some truths about myself, the work I do, and what it means. Maybe sharing them with you will help you reflect on your own life and uncover some of your own personal truths.

Here, in no special order, are a few of these nuggets of self-discovery.

SIX THINGS I LOVE

1. Being boss!—Thinking of stuff to do, and helping people do it.

2. Watching teachers teach, and teaching them to be better.

3. Planning my life and helping others to plan theirs.

4. Sitting and thinking, alone and with others.

5. Leisure and travel—yes, I love these as much as I love work.

6. Bouncing back from adversity.

SIX THINGS I HATE

1. Senseless meetings, long memos, and rigid rules.

2. Incompetent people who refuse to recognize and accept responsibility for their own incompetence.

3. Nonreflecting people—people who don't think about their practice and who don't question its effectiveness daily.

4. People who talk about "race pride" and "rescuing kids" but don't do the hard work needed to really help children of color.

5. The madness and jitters that infect adults and kids at certain times—just before holidays, and on rainy full-moon days.

6. The ends of things: a school term, a year, a friendship.

SEVEN THINGS I'VE DISCOVERED ABOUT THE WORK

1. Sometimes, God sends devils to move your destiny.

2. You must trust yourself and your instincts.

3. Reflecting daily on your efforts and outcomes helps to improve both.

4. You should accept tough assignments as challenges, and work like hell to succeed.

5. You get from others what you expect, demand, and model.

6. Working to be liked rather than respected diminishes your effectiveness.

7. Consistency and perseverance win out over running from fad to fad.

On the Heart of the Matter

We can reform society only if every place we live—every school, workplace, church, and family—becomes a site of reform.

~

As you grow, so does your work, and so will those whose lives you touch.

~

As you rise in any walk of life, never forget the nervousness of your first day—and how much you had to learn. You still do!

This Work of Teaching

WRITTEN UPON MY RETIREMENT AS
PRINCIPAL OF THE FREDERICK DOUGLASS
ACADEMY, SEPTEMBER 1995

To do this work of teaching and not feel at times its pervasive futility in the face of the reality of most children's lives, one would have to be heart dead. Yet when one has the calling, to refuse to do this work or to fail to do it well would be unconscionable.

When I began this work, I was naive. At twenty-one, I was energetic, hopeful, and not fully aware of the scope, influence, and power of teachers. I quickly had my eyes opened about just how broad my sphere of influence was. And I came to realize how frequently the power of school is misused. However, despite some jaded and cynical colleagues, some inept administrators, and some irreparably damaged children, I moved beyond being appalled at what I saw. I decided that my classroom (my program), my school, would constitute my queendom. Within this realm, I would do the best I knew how for children, for teachers, and for the community.

I leave this phase of my work holding on to energy and hope. I will continue working in education, buoyed up by the many children who have been rescued by my efforts and those of the incredibly driven staffs that I had.

I believe that the site of lasting reform must be every school. And I believe that the spirit-killing demons of poverty—unemployment, inadequate housing, and lack of health care—should make the work of creating effective schools for every child in this country the mission not just of educators but also of politicians and the powerful monied people who see the lives of the poor only from a vast and comfortable distance.

I move on, leaving this advice to my colleagues and comrades in this struggle to do the radical work of transforming poor kids' lives:

1. Take no prisoners.

2. Make no excuses.

3. Do whatever it takes.

4. Persevere.

5. Pray for guidance to do and say the right things daily.

6. Leave when you can no longer do and when you no longer believe that Nothing Is Impossible.

THE FREDERICK DOUGLASS ACADEMY
OFFICE OF THE PRINCIPAL

SEPTEMBER 11, 1995

Dear Staff,

With the exception of some programming difficulties, our school opening for the year was splendid. Each of you worked with our kids with the zeal that strikes to the heart of the matter, offering solid, challenging, interesting work that is on a par with the best that excellent public, private, and parochial schools deliver.

I have noted your concerns expressed during Friday's impromptu faculty meeting; together we will resolve them the same way we have resolved our mutual concerns in the past—with intelligence, pervasiveness of expectation, collegiality, and humor.

Many of my colleagues elsewhere in the school system are envious because of our accomplishments here. We know that these achievements are the result of hard work and deep belief in our kids. Press on!

I'll be around a lot. It gives me great joy to continue to watch you, help you, and support you. Have a great year.

L.M.

PublicAffairs is a new nonfiction publishing house and a tribute to the standards, values, and flair of three persons who have served as mentors to countless reporters, writers, editors, and book people of all kinds, including me.

I. F. Stone, proprietor of *I. F. Stone's Weekly*, combined a commitment to the First Amendment with entrepreneurial zeal and reporting skill and became one of the great independent journalists in American history. At the age of eighty, Izzy published *The Trial of Socrates*, which was a national bestseller. He wrote the book after he taught himself ancient Greek.

Benjamin C. Bradlee was for nearly thirty years the charismatic editorial leader of *The Washington Post*. It was Ben who gave the *Post* the range and courage to pursue such historic issues as Watergate. He supported his reporters with a tenacity that made them fearless, and it is no accident that so many became authors of influential, best-selling books.

Robert L. Bernstein, the chief executive of Random House for more than a quarter century, guided one of the nation's premier publishing houses. Bob was personally responsible for many books of political dissent and argument that challenged tyranny around the globe. He is also the founder and was the longtime chair of Human Rights Watch, one of the most respected human rights organizations in the world.

∿

For fifty years, the banner of Public Affairs Press was carried by its owner, Morris B. Schnapper, who published Gandhi, Nasser, Toynbee, Truman, and about 1,500 other authors. In 1983 Schnapper was described by *The Washington Post* as "a redoubtable gadfly." His legacy will endure in the books to come.

Peter Osnos, Publisher